Mountain Biking
Bald Eagle State Forest

Rob Ginieczki

Pennsylvania State Forest Series #1

Griz Guides are driven towards bringing the outdoor enthuaist the ultimate in user-friendly and highly accurate guidebooks. Each guide contains innovative approaches to displaying and relaying pertenent inofrmation to the user. All books were designed around GPS data for the utmost in accuracy. This includes painstakingly detailed GPS maps, highly explanitory written descriptions, tons of photos and other information necessary for a safe and enjoyable experience in the great outdoors. You can obtain extra copies of this guide or order other guides by the author by using the order form located in the rear of the book. You may also check out the website at www.grizguides.com

2002 © Griz Guides Publishing
Bucks County, Pennsyltucky

Cover Photo: Darius Mark styles it through the rock gardens.
Photographer: Nabil K. Mark Photography © 2008
www.NabilMark.com

All photos, drawings, slander and maps by
the author unless otherwise noted.

ISBN 0-9719681-0-1

Warning:
Outdoor recreation activities are by their very nature potentially hazardous. Anyone participating in these activities must assume responsibility for their own actions and safety. None of the information in this guide can replace sound judgement and solid decision-making abilkity of the user. The scope of this book does not reveal all potential risks and hazards of the activities listed herein. Learn as much as possible about your outdoor pursuits, prepare for the unexpected and be cautious. In the end you'll have a safer, enjoyable and more fun experience.

Dedication

To my Mom
Nancy
*for her perservering spirit,
endless support
and countless acts
of selfless love*

Thanks for being my 'Lighthouse'

ACKNOWLEDGEMENTS

The list is long but stacked with family n' friends both tried and true

-Karl Rosengarth for countless rides, stories, inspiration and guide assistance in the heart of Bald Eagle
-The folks at Dirt Rag Magazine for their friendship and support, especially the 'Art Guy' Jeff Guerrero.
-Jeff Lockwood @ Bittergravity.com for the killer site
-Dave Seasholtz, Bill Laubscher and Jay DeJesus for their friendship in the mountains and mellow nights 'round the campfire.
-Lori Woodring for many selfless shuttles, shared gourmet meals, great times, fantastic rides and memorable moments in the forest.
-District Forester Amy Griffith, Forester Karl Maul and Secretary Brenda for all of their help in answering my countless questions and requests from the Bald Eagle Sate Forest District Office.
-Mike McCourt for all his computer expertise and support
-Christie and Joe Del Ciotto and the Del Ciotto family for the tons of family and technical support
-Mom for use of her space, computer and moral support to make this all possible.
-To the advertisers that helped finance the printing of the guide, please support'em, they offer the serious goods!
-To all the dedicated folks in DCNR who continue to designate and maintain trails to play on for folks like us.
-My riding and climbing buddies who share a love and respect for natural places
-The Great Spirit for creating the wonderful and wild places that make me whole.

There is no death.
Only a changing of worlds.
Chief Seattle

Friends and family in the State Forest

INTRODUCTION

Regional Map and Map Legend...8-9
Cycles, Change and Access..10
Making sense of the guide..12
Duct Tape..18
Penns Woods..19
History of the Mountain Trails..23
Hunting Season..28
IMBA Rules and Giving Back..28-31

SOUTHERN BALD EAGLE STATE FOREST

1. Wildcat Gap to Faust Valley...34
2. Pine Swamp..39
3. Big Poe Mountain...42
4. Seven Mountains Enduro Epic..46
5. Penns Valley Rail Trail West...52
6. Penns Valley Rail Trail East..56
7. Tunnel Mountain Trail...60
8. Bull Hollow...65
9. Strong Mountain...68
10. Middle Ridge to Henstep Valley...73
11. Penns Creek Mountain...76
12. Booney Mountain..79
13. Shade Mountain...83

NORTHERN BALD EAGLE STATE FOREST

14. Round Top Mountain Lookout...90
15. Big Mountain..94
16. Bear Mountain...98
17. Hall Mountain Trail...102
18. Rapid Run Ramble..106

19. Hough Mountain Trail...109
20. Sharpback to Rocky Corner 113
21. Douty Mill Trail 118
22. Fallen Timber to Yankee Run...............................122
23. Boiling Springs..127
24. Cowbell Hollow...131
25. Old Tram Trail...135
26. Buffalo Mountain...139
27. Round Knob to Stony Gap....................................143
28. Mags Path to Black Gap......................................148
29. Heintz Trail to Swenks Gap.................................152
30. Spike Buck to Top Mountain.................................155
31. Dynamite Shack...159

SOUTHERN TIADAGHTON STATE FOREST

32. Southern Tiadaghton Tour.....................................166
33. Sand Spring Flat..173
34. Mountain Gap Trail..177

WILLIAMSPORT WATER AUTHORITY

35. Mosquito Valley...184
36. Raccoon Mountain...189
37. Heller Reservoir..193

APPENDIX

Griz Guide Sponsors..198-216
Camping Out...198-199
Bed & Breakfast Establishments...........................200-202
Bike Shops..203,207
Contact Information..204
Short List O'Rides..Griz Pic's....................................206
About the Author...209

Introduction

MAP LEGEND

Interstate		Stream	
Paved Road		Rail Trail	
Dirt Road		Pipeline	
Woods Road		Powerline	
Trail		Boundary	
Faint Trail		Bridge	
State Highway	⟨26⟩	Trailhead	
U.S. Highway	(322)	Fire Tower	
Interstate Highway	(I-80)	"Black Box"	33.6 3.6
State Road	SR 2012	Lake/Pond	
Township Road	T 487	Vista/View	
State Park	🌲	Gate	•—•
Natural Area	🌲	Campground	▲
Parking Area	🅿	Boulders	
Building/Cabin	🏠	Swamp	
Ruins	Ⓡ	Furnace	▲
Point of Interest	✪	Spring	
Mine/Gravel Pit	⚒	Bear	
Sketchy Descent	☠	Friendly Bears	
Heart Poundin' Hill	💓	Deer Fence Area	

REGIONAL MAP

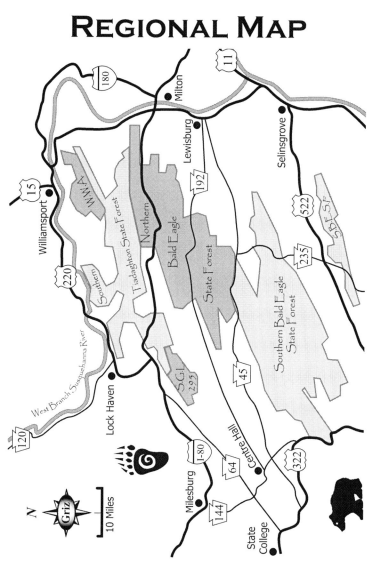

CYCLES AND CHANGE

No, this ain't about mountain bikes and shiny nickels, but the reality of life. I take big risks putting together a guidebook that, even before being printed, will inevitably change. Life is all about change and the roads and lands that this guidebook covers are no exception. The forest will continue to be logged, opening up new roads not shown on my maps and possibly forcing existing trails to be rerouted. Weather events like ice storms, windstorms, tornadoes and insect damage continue to take a toll on the trees and invariably the trails. After any of these events you may find a ride almost impassible. I do not manage the lands, DCNR holds that responsibility as do you as a Conservation Volunteer. Two words for you, "**Get Involved!**" Highways are always under construction and just as this book was being completed, Department of Transportation renumbered all highway exits statewide. Events like this shape our world so be prepared to deal with changes you will invariably find in the field. Remember that this guide, as painstakingly put together and accurate as it may be, is only a guide. Wanna contribute? Wanna find out about any changes in the field, **FREE UPDATES** and downloads: **www.grizguides.com** Check it out!

ACCESS

Access is an ever-growing issue in Pennsylvania. More and more people are getting out and enjoying the woods and old-school, narrow-minded user groups are not taking to this too kindly. The Keystone Trail Association (KTA) is one of these groups that has developed an extremist attitude to trail ownership on state lands. Granted that the miles of singletrack trail they have built as an organization should remain for foot-travel only, but take away logger, miner and Indian pathways and they wouldn't have much of trail system at all! After all, the land that "their" trail is built on is every Pennsylvania taxpayer's land. Two frightening examples: The Mid-State Trail hikers of the KTA were cryin' over the fact that the Central Mountain Trail was run on a small section of logging road that is also part of the Mid-State Trail (*Ride # 32 Sand Spring Flat*). In an immature fashion, the KTA responded by covering over their orange-blazed trail with brown stain. Sorry folks! If it weren't for the loggers' way back when, you wouldn't even have a trail to hike on. Second example was a published writing in the KTA newsletter during the 'blaze-covering' events, by the KTA head honcho Tom, stating that " mountain bikers and equestrians ruin my wilderness experience". Geeze, this boy needs to wake-up and realize he's not in Kansas anymore or interior Alaska for that matter. Fact is the East Coast is growing every day and so are the groups of folks getting out to recreate in the woods. I'm thinking Tom and the KTA folks need to get a life!

Fortunately DCNR and the insightful folks at the Bald Eagle State Forest have the foresight to see that outdoor recreation is growing beyond the traditional hiker. They have made massive strides to include other trail user groups including mountain bikers. So what does this mean for you and me and the future of our sport? One word stands strong against close-minded groups like the KTA and bureaucrat politicians in state offices, **Volunteer Hours**. The man-hours we can invest as a group will introduce, improve and maintain our image amongst ourselves and the world at large. I personally have logged countless hours of trail work in State Forests and State Parks. It is time for you to help join the handful of us that bear the load. The scary reality is that the state holds the power to close many or all of the incredible trails in this guide and throughout the state. Do your part to help and **Volunteer Hours Today!** Contact the following groups listed in the appendix for more information on how you can help.

The earth is the mother of all people, and all people should have equal rights upon it. You might as well expect the rivers to run backwards as that any man who was born free should be contented when penned up and denied liberty to go where he pleases.

Chief Joseph, Nez Perce

HOW TO USE THE GUIDE

"Fat Free Guarantee"

I have designed this guide to be as informative as possible yet 'fat-free'. Too many guides are filled with bogus crap and extraneous 'stuff' that makes for a heavier and confusing text. These books are also known as 'Certified Grade "A" Bullshit' books. One bogus item you <u>won't</u> find in this guide are elevation profiles. In their place are listed a **Vertical** and **Climbing Distance** heading. After talking with many riding folks from all walks, I found that most people don't even know how to interpret an elevation profile, let alone use it to help them find their way on a ride. These graphs or charts are basically a waste of paper better left out for quality pictures and a more trail-friendly sized guide. Most riders rely on GPS accurate maps with printed mileage, a detailed mileage log and the total amount and length of climbing encountered on the ride (found in the **Vertical** and **Climbing Distance** headings). All of this is found in my guide. One user-friendly feature you will find in this guide is the **Black Box** mileage markers on the GPS digital maps. This **Black Box** feature is critical in linking the text in the mileage log to the actual location on the map. Enjoy these features that set my guidebooks apart from the rest!

The guide is arranged into four separate regions: *Southern Bald Eagle State Forest, Northern Bald Eagle State Forest, Southern Tiadaghton State Forest and the Williamsport Water Authority*. The format has been carefully designed to offer you the most important information needed to evaluate, assess, locate, successfully complete and enjoy each ride. This guide will not fix your flat, pedal your bike or save you from a sketchy encounter with an irate black bear. My sole purpose is to give you the foundation for an informative yet adventurous experience in the beautiful Penns Woods while testing your personal mettle on a mountain bike.

NAVIGATING THE GUIDE...

Ride number and name: For ease of referencing, the rides have been numbered and named. The numbers follow sequence from southwest to northeast. The names of the rides come from a variety of sources: specific trails traversed during the ride, a mountain or valley the ride passes through, or some long-time local name.

Trailhead: This section tells you how far the ride is from a prominent town and how to get there with accurate driving directions. The Bald Eagle State Forest public use map and the Pennsylvania Atlas and Gazetteer are indispensable map tools that will assist you greatly in finding the trailhead. More importantly, these maps can be marked so that you can find that killer ride trailhead again. G.P.S. waypoints are listed for techno-winnies!

Distance: The length of the ride in miles and the type of ride (loop, out and back or one way). Each ride has been tediously mapped with GPS equipment for the utmost in accuracy.

Time: A rough estimate of the time needed to complete the ride. This basic figure is based on a non-stop ride at a pace of 5-7 miles an hour. The estimate does not include time for rest stops or exploration of other cool stuff encountered along the trail. Many rides have awesome highlights that demand your curiosity, so plan for it. Conditional factors can greatly influence a ride time. Sudden weather changes, poor trail conditions, mechanicals and injuries are just a few of the adversities you may face. Be prepared!

Highlights: A short list of cool natural and man-made features along the ride.

Technical Difficulty: Rated on a scale of Grades 1-5, Grade 5 being most difficult. This section helps you choose a ride that is within your technical riding ability. The Central Pennsylvania Mountains are home to some of the rockiest and technical riding in all of Pennsylvania. Bony ridgetops are often encountered and the valley tram grades are just as rocky and challenging. The objective rating is a combination of the type of obstacles encountered and their frequency along the route. The hardest section of the trail may not give the ride it's overall rating, especially if the rest of the ride is substantially less challenging. Some rides have very difficult technical sections of trail that are short and easily hiked through. The guide lists these small areas of substantially difficult terrain and their appropriate rating. The following is a numerical rating list:

Grade 1: Smooth to bumpy tread on dirt road type surfaces. Easily negotiated by riders of all levels and abilities.

Grade 2: Irregular terrain surfaces with more bumps and the occasional section of loose sand, dirt or gravel surfaces. Rideable lines are very evident.

Grade 3: Irregular terrains with a few rough sections of rocks, roots, logs and loose tread surfaces. May include short but steep climbs and descents. Rideable lines are more readily recognized along the trail.

Grade 4: Rough terrain with few smooth areas. More obscure lines through technical singletrack. Contains a diversity of terrain from rocks, roots, logs, bridges, water-bars, tight bar-grabbing singletrack, loose ground and off-camber trail. Steeper terrain prevails. Hiking may be required by less skilled riders.

Grade 5: Sustained sections of extreme technical difficulties with many dangerous trail hazards. Rideable lines are obscure or flat-out absent. Rock gardens, huge timber, dangerously loose descents and hair-raising off-camber trails are just a few of the extreme encounters.

Action Fotos

(real-life crashes! No riders were physically injured, although I can't comment on egos or the bushes)

Aerobic Difficulty: Mountain biking and aerobic difficulty go hand-in-hand. The idea of horsing around a 25+ pound bike through the woods can be downright difficult. Some hill climbs will have your heart throbbing and the flats will require finesse. Remember, this is ridge and valley country and there ain't no ski lifts to take you to the top! Due to individuals fitness levels of each rider, this may be one of the hardest categories to rate so use it as a basic guideline. This objective rating has been divided into three categories below:

Easy: Generally flat terrain with some gentle rolling hills.
Moderate: Climbs with short and sometimes steep grades. Some gradual grade climbs may be lengthy. Usually contains challenging terrain that requires extra effort.
Strenuous: Multiple and sustained climbs over steep terrain. Burly sections of demanding technical singletrack. Demands a high level of cardiac fitness, endurance and power.

SRAMless...Limping home, Singlespeed style

Vertical: This section describes the <u>total</u> amount of vertical feet ascended during the <u>entire</u> ride. What that means is that every time you ride up a hill, the number of vertical feet ascended is added to form the number listed here. The higher the number, the more climbing you will encounter on the ride. Easier grade rides typically fall under the 1,000 foot range. Rides of moderate grades typically fall in the 1,000 to 1,500 foot range. Rides that fall in the 2,000+ foot range are usually more strenuous and severe in grade. Use this number along with the technical and aerobic ratings to assist in choosing a ride.

Climbing Distance: This number, shown in miles, reflects the total distance spent climbing throughout the ride. Typically this number is higher than half of the rides total distance. This is due to climbs typically taking place on less-steep but longer grades.

Maps: This section lists the extra maps available to assist you in completing, extending or bailing-out of your intended ride. Much of the guide references the DCNR Bald Eagle State Forest Public Use Map and the Central Mountain Trail Public Use Map. This map is currently free to the public by contacting the DCNR Bald Eagle State Forest office at 570-922-3344.

Land Status: A listing of property owners or agencies that own or manage the land on which the ride travels. Much of the guide is within the Bald Eagle State Forest.

Ride Notes: A brief armchair tour of the blood, sweat and gears on the ride. A vivid picture is painted of the ride experience by listing historical, geologic, landmark and folklore information. Occasionally ride options are listed.

The Ride: This scroll of numbers is a detailed GPS mileage log. This highly accurate listing will assist you in finding the proper turns on the trail and keep you on track. A computerized bike odometer is a great tool to have and very handy when used with this guide. Make sure your computer is properly calibrated so that it is as accurate as possible. A GPS unit is not necessary but in the hands of a skilled user, becomes a complimentary route-finding tool. All readings are recorded to the one-tenth of a mile. Short, highly descriptive text explains what to look for and where to turn along the way. Use this rating in conjunction with the **Black Box** feature found on the **Route Maps** to easily find your way through a ride.

Route Maps: All route maps have been digitally drawn with extreme GPS accuracy. The maps are drawn to scale and include a mileage scale bar and compass. The maps also have a very exclusive feature, the **Black Box**, a visual mileage marker is placed at key intersections. The small **Black Box** notes the mileage at a given intersection to assist you in coordinating the mileage log with the map. This makes for a more accurate, simplified and user-friendly guide. Navigation-savvy riders could use the maps exclusively to follow the ride. Certain non-essential information has been left out for map clarity and quality. The ride route has been highlighted and directional arrows are included for extra clarity. All features drawn on the maps can be referenced in the front of the book on the **Map Legend** page. The maps were created this way in an attempt to keep them as clean and uncluttered as possible.

Karlos says "If it don't pedal, Duct Tape it!"

DUCT TAPE

Give praise to the almighty silver-sided duct tape! There isn't a more versatile 'tool' out there that works better than duct tape. Duct tape has bailed my butt outta more situations in the backcountry than I care to remember and I could probably write an entire book about the stuff. This multi-purpose adhesive is great for anything from small sidewall cuts to jerry-rigging a broken derailuer or closing a serious gash in your calf. Carry some with you by wrapping a sizeable length around your pump, seatpost, frame or a body part of choice. I've listed a few other basic items of importance to have along on your ride;

- **compact pump** (to reinflate your ego after that gnarly rock garden just kicked your ass)
- **spare tube** (for the first snake-bite)
- **patch kit** (for the next few snake-bites)
- **tire levers** (works great with duct-tape for traction splints on broken fingers).

It helps to have these items but it helps even more when you know how to use them! Get schooled on changing flats so you'll know what to do in the woods. Other items worth having are a multi-purpose tool, a first aid kit, some bailing wire and cable ties. Again, any tool is useless in the hands of the uneducated. These basic tools and the knowledge to use them have saved alota folks from a long hike outta the backwoods. If you find youself stuck and stranded while riding in the woods, remember this: The Native Indians believed that, with time, anywhere in Penns Woods is within walking distance.

The soil you see is not ordinary soil-it is the dust of the blood, the flesh, and the bones of our ancestors... You will have to dig down through the surface before you can find nature's earth, as the upper portion is Crow. The land, as it is, is my blood and my dead, it is consecrated...
                                        Shes-his, Reno Crow

PENNS WOODS

Native tribes of people have lived throughout this region for thousands of years. They fished the rivers, hunted the hills, farmed the fertile valleys and existed in harmony with the land. As settlers came from the East, these tribes were slowly cheated and forced from their sacred lands. As the white man moved westward, forts and towns sprung up throughout the region.

The most important change to Penns Woods came with the logging and mining eras. It was during the late 1800's and into the early 1900's that men headed into dark drainages to cut Hemlock for the tanning industry. The original logging practices actually never really harvested the trees but instead their thick bark rich in tannin. When wood became a bigger commodity than bark, logging companies headed deeper into the hills. As the logging industry progressed, the mules, streams and men were not fast enough to move timber from mountain to mill. In came the era of the logging railroad and tram grades. Small steel rails were being run through many of the hollows in the region. Strip mining for iron-ore was occurring west of here while shaft mining for coal was occurring in the east. The mining industries needed support from the timber companies. From this point forward, the history of the mountain trails begins.

The woods are filled with many wonderful things, some of which can hurt you. The forests hold some inherent dangers that most folks are unaware of. Water is everywhere in the forest, and in some cases the springs are as pure as you can get. But not all water is safe and every source should be considered suspect and treated. Animals are wild and sometimes unpredictable. Rabid raccoons, bluffing bears and feisty rattlesnakes are just a few of the encounters I've had out on the trail. Lighting on ridge-tops is a serious concern during spring and fall storms. Tornadoes have sprung up across the state although none have been documented in this region. Use the map to get you back to the trailhead when weather turns. Weather can and does change drastically in these hills and storms sometimes sneak up on you. Due to many years of heavy insect damage in this area, many dead oak trees stand throughout the region. Heavy winds can snap large branches or cause whole trees to break or uproot. Windstorms can be downright deadly with the size of many of these standing snags so avoid riding in these conditions.

Pennsylvania is home to many incredible tracts of state land. The lands covered in the guide are comprised of State Forest, State Parks, and State Game Lands. The State Forests comprise the bulk of the riding terrain and offer endless miles of outdoor exploration. Managed by the Department of Conservation and Natural Resources, these state lands offer everything from hunting and fishing to horseback riding and snowmobiling. The Bald Eagle State Forest is almost 200,000 acres in size and extends over 5 counties in the center part of the state. The forest derived it's name from the famous Pennsylvania Indian Chief 'Bald Eagle' and was the last stronghold of the mountain buffalo in the state of Pennsylvania. Sandstone ridges and limestone valleys comprise the geologic makeup and numerous hardwood and softwood tree species cloak these rolling ridges.

Seven State Parks can be found within or adjoining the Bald Eagle State Forest and their information is listed in the Camping section of the Appendix. Ten Natural and Wild Areas can be found within the forest highlighting unique biologic, geologic and historic regions. These areas have been set aside to protect the undeveloped character of the area and allow us to explore these special places that see little human impact. From bone-white outcrops of Tuscarora sandstone to high mountain swamps of cranberry and blueberry, Bald Eagle is home to many special places. Below is a list of the Wild and Natural Areas within the Bald Eagle and the highlights of the particular spot (this information is taken from the Bald Eagle State Forest Public Use Map):

Bear Run Natural Area: A 32-acre community of old growth hemlock, birch, yellow poplar and ash located south of Woodward.
Joyce Kilmer Natural Area: 77-acre tract of old growth white pine and hemlock located west of Hartleton.

Halfway Natural Area: 407-acre tract of mixed hardwoods and 'pingo scars' which are small depressions left from glacier activity. It is located due east of R.B. Winter State Park, up behind the campground.

Hook Natural Area: 5,119-acre tract preserving a complete watershed and home to rugged hiking trails located north of Hartleton.

Mt. Logan Natural Area: 512-acre tract of old growth hemlock and a cool outcrop of Tuscarora sandstone located east of Castanea.

Rosencrans Bog Natural Area: 152 acres of high mountain swamp with cranberry, mountain holly and high-bush blueberry located north of Loganton.

Snyder-Middleswarth Natural Area: 500-acre tract containing old growth hemlock, white pine and pitch pine. Many hiking trails access this area that was preserved by a state-ordered cutting ban in 1902. It is located 5 miles west of Troxelville and is also the trailhead for *Ride # 8 Bull Hollow*.

Tall Timbers Natural Area: 660-acre tract of second growth oak, white pine and hemlock with many hiking trails. It is adjacent (just west of) to the Snyder-Middleswarth Natural Area.

White Mountain Wild Area: 3,581-acre tract encompasses most of White Mountain which derives its name from the massive Tuscarora sandstone talus fields on both the north and south slopes. After hiking through this awesome place, I can attest to a true 'wilderness' experience. It is located southwest of Weikert.

Mohn Mill Ponds Wild Plant Sanctuary: 381-acre tract of mixed oaks amongst vernal ponds and springs. The two-mile long Merrill Lynn Trail circles this awesome area located on the tri-county border of Clinton, Lycoming and Union counties. *Ride # 31, Dynamite Shack*, passes this special place.

Introduction

In an effort to manage the biodiversity of plant species in the forest understory, there are many deer fence projects in place. An example of these is found along *Ride # 4 Seven Mountains Enduro Epic*, where the trail passes through one of these gated enclosures.

Bald Eagle isn't the only State Forest showcased in this guide. The southern section of Tiadaghton State Forest has many of its own treasures. Tiadaghton holds many of the same features found in Bald Eagle, including many old logging tram grades. These old grades make for excellent riding and stand as a testament to the hard work of loggers long ago. The southern section of Tiadaghton State Forest has little in the way of natural and wild areas but holds one small but special State Park. Ravensburg State Park is located in a deep gap below towering chossy cliffs in a beautifully rugged location. The small dam sets the scene for tranquil outing (except for the roaring traffic on State Highway 880!). This location is an ideal day-use area with excellent picnic pavilions, playground, hiking, and even a bit of moderate rock climbing. Although there are no rides that leave from this exact location, Ravensburg State Park is a worthy stop if you're in the area riding *Rides 32-34*. The forest delineation line between Bald Eagle and Tiadaghton State Forests runs more or less along the county line between Lycoming and Union Counties, north of Interstate 80.

The Williamsport Water Authority is truly a hidden sanctuary for wildlife and outdoor folk alike. This huge tract of preserved and protected lands ensures a safe and clean water source for the nearby metropolis of Williamsport. Only minuets outta town, this preserve is home to many of our native animals and plenty of them. The area was a small farming community at one time and many house foundations in the woods still remain. One of the service roads that leads out to Mosquito Valley Reservoir follows the original highway that connected Williamsport with towns south. An old stone highway mile-marker stands as proof of this ancient byway. *Rides 35-37* explore the neat finds in this special place.

HISTORY OF THE MOUNTAIN TRAILS

It probably all started back with the native and Indigenous peoples that once roamed these hills. Evidence of these past cultures is found today in the silty riverbanks, farm fields and the names of some area towns. Some of these Native footpaths that remained were then utilized by the settlers who began to explore this dark, forested region. As time passed on and more folks moved across the land, the trails grew into roads and highways as we know them today. The history of many of the trails in this guide are quite interesting, so I've included some information on how they came to be the awesome rides as you find them today.

Not much is recorded about the early indigenous peoples but as time wore on, the events in the region became increasingly documented. With the disruption of the Native Indians, the settlers pushed into different regions of the state and began exploring different natural resources. Logging and mining Pennsylvania's natural resources became a profitable and industrious business that grew out of much hard work and a lot of creativity. Many of the first mining and logging practices were developed right here in Pennsylvania.

The central mountain region of the state wasn't dubbed the

The men, machines and materials that formed the trails
Reprinted with permission, Pennsylvania R.R. Museum

23

Introduction

"heartland" for nothing. Ancient trees lined both valley and hill making for a vast supply of timber and timber products. It wasn't the timber that the loggers originally had in mind but the thick bark of the hemlock tree. This thick bark was vital to the tanning industry because the bark was rich in tannin. Tannin was used in the leather tanning process for tanning hides.

Wood became a bigger commodity than bark and the logging companies headed deeper into the high hills and dark valleys. At first men carved narrow grades into the hillsides so that the mule teams could skid the logs down to the creeks below. The logs were then sent by waterway to the mills in big towns like Williamsport. On the murky bottom of the Susquehanna River, adjacent to town, lie the remains of log cribs. These wooden 'cribs' helped contain the masses of logs that were floated down the mighty Susquehanna from points upstream. It was these original footpaths and skidder grades that began to shape the trails we use today.

As the logging progressed, mules, streams and men were not fast enough to move timber from mountain to mill. With lumber higher and deeper in the hills, this less accessible wood needed to be attained by a better system. With this goal in mind the era of the logging railroad and tram grades began. The Bald Eagle area was especially influential in using the early methods of rail travel to acquire this timber. The streams in the Bald Eagle region were too small to float timber to larger watercourses and they generally flowed in the wrong direction towards the major mills.

The era of 'Wild-Catting' began with timber work crews that would construct narrow grades on the mountain. They would dig out the grade, sometimes line it with ballast (rock), lay down rough timber ties and fasten hardwood or small steel rails. Their rough construction was sketchy at best and this primitive form of logging was quite risky. It's hard to imagine tons of timber being run down a mountain on a wooden-railed railroad! Many of these tramways were built up through the numerous hollows in the region. "Wild Catting" was a logging technique by which logs were transported by a set of log 'trucks' and run by gravity to the mills. Originally horses towed the log trucks up the railway to the log landing. The log trucks consisted of two sets of steel flanged wheels attached to a frame. Once towed up the railway to a log landing, the pair of trucks were then loaded by hand. The logs were then fastened to the trucks with chain and a "Wild-Catter" would then ride the truck back down the mountain to the mill.

Many horses were killed from runaway log 'trucks' that killed them on their climb up the grade. Small locomotive trains replaced the horses that hauled empty log trucks back up the mountain. "Wild-Catters" were also in a risky position, as these were the hardcore men who rode the log 'trucks' down the hill, controlling their speed with a hand brake. Steep grades, shifting loads, sketchy rails, high speeds and sharp turns were part of the inherent danger. With the help of gravity, some Wildcat trucks would reach speeds of 40 mph! Combine all this with the fact that many "Wildcat" trucks did not have suspension and you're looking at one hell of a ride!

With the change from mule to locomotive, the tramways continued to grow up remote hollows and over tall mountains. The locomotives eventually replaced the 'Wildcat' method by bringing the lumber 'trucks' down from the mountains, ending this exciting but hairy logging technique. Many of the rides in the Northern Bald Eagle and Southern Tiadaghton State Forests follow these historic "Wild-catting" tramways.

Inclines like the *Mags Path to Black Gap, Ride# 28* and the south

Joe sizing up a 500+ year-old Hemlock tree, and the view he experiences looking up into this Eastern giant.

25

side of Hall Mountain on the *Hall Mountain Trail, Ride # 17* show you just how steep some of these grades can get. *The Old Tram Trail, Ride # 25*, northeast of R.B. Winter State Park, is an excellent example of an old tram railway. The huge ballast rocks still pave a relatively flat surface that the timber ties once sat upon. This tram grade although challenging and difficult to ride on, is probably one of the best preserved of its type, in the region.

Hard, black Anthracite coal was discovered in the northeastern section of the state and with that began the mining boom. This 'black gold' is considered some of the finest coal in the world and much of it was used to fuel the growing industrial era. Although there weren't any coal mines in the Bald Eagle region, the forests here supported the mining industry with 'prop timber' used in propping the rock ceiling of the coal mine veins. Much of the timber logged in the Northern Bald Eagle State Forest was used for props. The southern sections of the forest held more prized timber, which was used for bark and boards.

With the fall of the lumbering era, the forests were barren and littered with treetops. The Commonwealth took advantage of these 'waste-lands' and purchased them from logging companies' dirt-cheap. The state organization of Forests and Waters was in charge of maintaining these newly acquired parcels. As the forests regenerated new growth, many changes occurred. Many mountains in Pennsylvania experienced massive fires from the logging slash. During the Roosevelt term, many young fellas were employed under the CCC organization. They built numerous 'fire-line' trails. These trails are typically the ones that run straight up and over the mountains in a north-south direction. Since these mountains run in a basic west to east direction, many of the fire-line trails were designed to run perpendicular to the ridges. In this way an advancing fire that would typically travel east, could be stopped at one of many 'fire-line' trails. The CCC boys also built many of the rugged picnic pavilions and small rock dams found at many of the State Parks. They were very instrumental in designing many of the facilities in the State Parks during this time.

The story continues with ongoing forest activity in the Central Pennsylvania Mountains. Logging has changed a lot since the early 1900 exploits. Today foresters' 'cruise' timber stands, marking select trees to be cut. A variety of trees remain in the timbered areas for habitat, reseeding and aesthetics. This selective cutting process helps maintain a healthy forest plus provides a scant income for the State Forests. The logging efforts also work to maintain the old roads and the state has passed a measure to preserve the existing state-designated hiking trails by preventing logging within 100 feet of established trail. Although this does not apply to any of the trails in this guide, the awesome folks at DCNR have vowed to maintain the integrity of all trails published in their maps, which also happens to include most of the trails in this guide. Rest assured that the DCNR continues to place recreation at the forefront of their long-range goals as managers of our beautiful forests.

The trail history is still unfolding today as more and more folks head into State Forests. Hikers, horse riders and **mountain bikers** are now becoming an integral part of the forest's history. With the help of the DCNR and more importantly the Bald Eagle State Forest District, the Central Mountain Trail was developed in 2001. With input from three user groups (bikers, hikers and horse riders), Bald Eagle put together the most expansive and incredible public use, multi-use trail to date. This incredible network of trail is covered in many of the rides in this guide. The Bald Eagle has set an outstanding standard for recreation trail among all the State Forest Districts. The future of these trails depends on all user groups to help maintain their integrity. You can be a part of the unwritten history by contacting the Bald Eagle State Forest District office to request information on how to become a conservation volunteer. The Bald Eagle District office may also be able to provide information on when groups are planning work weekends to ride, hike, bike and maintain the trail. See the Appendix for contact information.

HUNTING SEASON

Hunting season in Pennsylvania is an active time in many of our State Forests, Parks and Game Lands. Mountain bikers wishing to ride during the annual hunting season should take precautions while in the woods. Deer season with a gun is typically the most dangerous time to be in the woods riding a bike. The season start date changes from year to year but typically begins on the first Monday after Thanksgiving and runs for two weeks. It is best to wear bright (florescent orange) colors and make yourself seen and heard while riding. <u>Better yet, don't risk your life and give the hunters a break by riding elsewhere during the deer season</u>. Due to constant changes in the hunting seasons, it is best to contact the Pennsylvania Game Commission to update yourself with current information. Don't be a statistic!

IMBA RULES OF THE TRAIL

In the prophetic words of my friend Marc Taylor, "Roots, Rock, Respect" says a lot about mountain biking. I hang heavily on the last one, "Respect". Many of our trail issues and concerns stem from this one all-encompassing word. Respect other trail users, they have just as much of a right to be out on the trail as you. Respect the land. Skid-marks (no, not the kind in your underwear!), tire tracks in muddy trail and other forms of erosion remain to been seen by others, long after you finish your ride. Each one of us stands for all of us in the eyes of 'Joe Public', **THINK!**

1. Ride on open trails only. Respect trail and road closures, avoid trespassing on private land and obtain permits and authorization needed to access land. The way you ride will influence trail management decisions and policies.

2. Leave no trace. The soils in this rocky region are sensitive. Be aware that riding after heavy rains could cause serious impact. Some trails may be muddy and are unavoidable, stay on the trail and do not create new ones. Practice low-impact cycling. Pack out at least as much as you pack in!

3. Control your bike. Be cognoscente (aware) of other trail users on blind turns and hilly terrain.

4. Always yield trail. Give other trail users plenty of advance notice of your intent to cautiously pass. A handlebar-mounted bell works great as a mellow greeting and is not startling. Show respect by passing slowly, walking or stopping, especially around horses. Remember that the folks you meet out there are looking to get away from it all and have a good time, just like you.

5. Don't scare animals. All animals are instinctively startled by sudden movement and loud noises. This causes animals to react in a compulsive manner, causing harm to the animal, others and you. Give animals extra berth and time to adjust to your presence. When passing horses, be extra careful and communicate with the rider on how they would like you to pass.

6. Plan ahead. Know your equipment, ability and the region in which you are riding so that you can prepare properly. Be self-sufficient at all times, keep your equipment in good repair and carry all necessary supplies to repair you and your bike. Be aware of weather changes and change plans accordingly. A well-planned trip should be an enjoyment to you and your buds, not a burden to Search and Rescue. Always wear a helmet.

Approaching hikers with care

Multi-use icon on the CMT

Griz Guides is a member of and proudly supports these organizations which all share the common goal to create, enhance and preserve trail opportunities locally and globally, for mountain bikers. Share in the fun, become an IMBA member and join an IMBA club today!

Griz Guides pledges 1% of all guidebook sales to Pennsylvania IMBA Organizations. By purchasing this guidebook, you've indirectly begun to help trail access, maintenance and building across the Keystone State. The future of mountain biking in Pennsylvania depends on the direct action of all riders. Contact your regional IMBA representative today to see what you can do today to help the future of our trails tomorrow.

Visit *www.imba.com* and go to *Contacts/Links* to find the Pennsylvania Representative or affiliated IMBA club in your region.

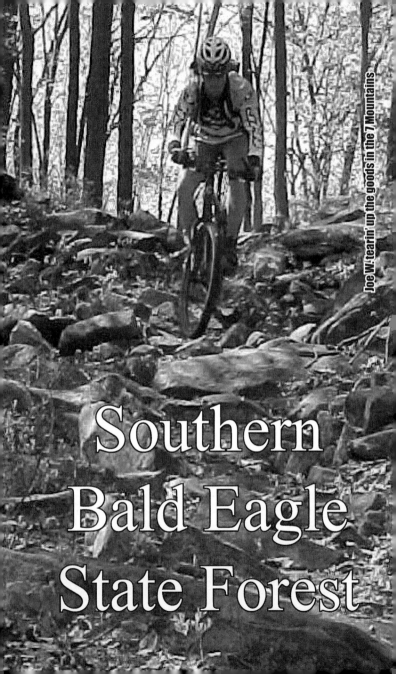

Joe W. tearin' up the goods in the 7 Mountains

Southern Bald Eagle State Forest

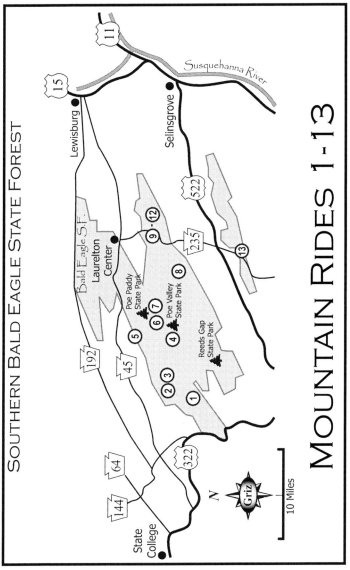

SOUTHERN BALD EAGLE STATE FOREST

MOUNTAIN RIDES 1-13

WILDCAT GAP TO FAUST VALLEY
RIDE 1

Trailhead: Sand Mountain and Millheim Pike Roads, 21 miles from State College. From State College, travel east on U.S. 322 to Potters Mills. After passing Potters Mills, the highway will soon turn to a 4-lane expressway. Once on the expressway turn left at the second left turn on to Sand Mountain Road, at the large brown sign stating 'Poe Valley State Park'. Carefully follow this windy road 5.8 miles to just before the T intersection with Millheim Pike. Turn right on this unnamed gravel spur road and park along the edge of the road. The ride begins at the intersection of Sand Mountain Road and the unnamed spur road. **GPS**: N40-47.640' W77-31.540'

Distance: 7.4 mile loop

Time: 1-2 hours

Highlights: Scintillating singletrack, excellent energetic beginner ride, travels through the 'heart' of the *Seven Mountains Enduro Epic route (Ride # 4),* beautiful backcountry beaver pond.

Technical Difficulty: **2+**. The final section of singletrack along the north edge of Sand Mountain Ridge presents the greatest challenge with a heavier dose of rock-covered trail. Most riders can pedal through the tougher sections if they remember that momentum is their friend.

Aerobic Difficulty: **Easy to Moderate**. With the short climbing sections at the mid-point of the ride, the loop generally follows a gentle roll as it picks it's way through the woods.

Vertical: 829 feet of climbing

Climbing Distance: 3.9 miles

Maps: DCNR Bald Eagle State Forest Public Use Map.

Land Status: DCNR Bald Eagle State Forest

Ride Notes: You say you want the best of southern Bald Eagle State Forest singletrack but you're not up to the Seven Mountains Enduro Epic loop of epic size? Welcome to the honey pot! This ride covers

Mountain Biking Bald Eagle State Forest
Griz Guides

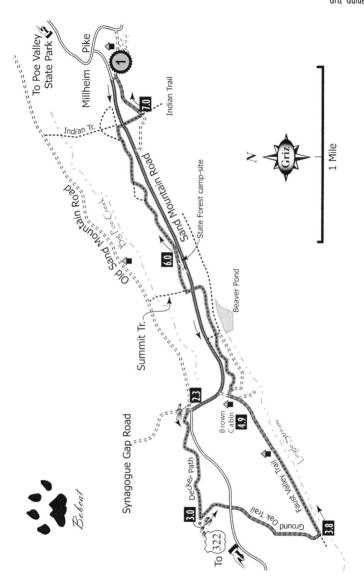

To Poe Valley State Park

Millheim Pike

Indian Trail

Indian Tr.

Big Poe Creek

Old Sand Mountain Road

Sand Mountain Road

State Forest camp-site

Beaver Pond

Summit Tr.

Synagogue Gap Road

Decker Path

Brown Cabin

Ground Oak Trail

Faust Valley Trail

Little Stream

To 322

1

7.0

6.0

2.3

4.9

3.0

3.8

N

Griz

1 Mile

Bobcat

35

the core goods of the bigger loop but leaves out the hellacious hills and menacing miles. You will ride the first half of the loop on forest roads and the back-half on singletrack. Designed as a Dual Sport dirt bike trail system, the singletrack sections are blazed yellow in the opposite direction of travel so you might check over your shoulder occasionally to make sure you're on route.

Beginning at a spur-road trailhead, the ride begins a slow climb out to the unique intersection of Sand Mountain, Synagogue Gap and Old Sand Mountain Roads. From here a devious singletrack awaits, luring you up and over Sand Mountain Road again. The descent terminates on the Faust Valley Trail, an old logging railroad grade, where local lure claims the wreckage of an old "iron horse" lies just off this grade in the woods. As the trail turns from singletrack to doubletrack, another snappy series of turns leads through fragrant pines and runs out above the beautiful backcountry beaver pond. Jumping back over to Sand Mountain Road, the more rugged stretch of singletrack is traversed as the Indian Trail dumps you back down on yet another old logging railroad grade. This spongy green carpet runs the valley back to the trailhead.

THE RIDE...

0.0 From the trailhead parking area, ride out to Sand Mountain Road and turn left on Sand Mountain Road.

2.3 At this interesting intersection of Sand Mountain, Synagogue Gap and Old Sand Mountain Roads, bear right on Synagogue Gap Road and immediately after turn left on a singletrack trail, the Decker Path, in the woods. At mile 3.0 the trail will turn 90 degrees left, cross a small rock pile and climb sharply.

3.2 Cross Sand Mountain Road and descend the Ground Oak Trail 4-wheel drive road.

3.8 Turn left at the T intersection on to the Faust Valley Trail. Rumor has it that somewhere along this old railroad grade lies the remains of an old iron logging locomotive.

4.9 Turn right on to the woods road, just opposite a driveway leading to a brown cabin. This is the second woods road on the right and if you arrive at Sand Mountain Road, you missed the turn. Immediately after the turn, turn left on to a wide singletrack that leads into a stand of pines. Look on the back of trees to find the yellow blazes.

5.2 Cross a 4-way singletrack intersection above a beautiful backcountry beaver pond, check it out if you have time! Continue straight on the singletrack that runs parallel along Sand Mountain Road.

5.7 Cross Sand Mountain Road on to the Summit Trail, marked by the wooden sign. Once in the woods at the crest of the hill, turn right on to the right spur trail. DO NOT follow the Summit Trail and blue blazes straight down over the ridge. Soon after (mile 6.0), the trail comes out to a grassy woods road, passes a State Forest campsite and fire ring on the left. Approximately 50 feet before the grassy woods road merges with Sand Mountain Road, turn left on to

The tranquil beaver pond on Sand Mountain

the sandy singletrack. Soon you will come to a fork, keep right at the fork, unless you want to visit a small vista via a sharp descent/ascent.

6.8 Keep right at a fork, soon after turning right on the blue-blazed Indian Trail. If you take the left fork at this intersection, the trail drops down a steep tram grade, cross the blue blazed Indian Trail and reascends the tram grade. Soon after the trail loops back and turns left on to the Indian Trail, blazed blue. The Indian Trail will descend, crossing Sand Mountain Road.

7.0 Turn left at the T intersection on to the spongy moss-covered woods road.

7.4 Turn left on the gravel road and arrive at the trailhead.

Copperhead

PINE SWAMP
RIDE 2

Trailhead: **Mountain Church and Millheim Pike Roads**, 23 miles from State College. From State College, travel east on U.S. 322 to Potters Mills. After passing Potters Mills, the highway will soon turn to a 4-lane expressway. Once on the expressway turn left at the second left turn, at the large brown sign stating 'Poe Valley State Park', on to Sand Mountain Road. Carefully follow this windy road 6 miles to a T intersection with Millheim Pike. Turn left on Millheim Pike and follow the road down the hill 1 mile. At the bottom of the hill, the road will become paved. Turn left at the fork on the gravel road, which is still Millheim Pike and climb the steep hill 1 mile. At the summit of the hill, Mountain Church Road will intersect with Millheim Pike. Park here in the large pull-out area on the right and the ride begins at this intersection. **GPS**: N40-49.111' W77-30.056'

Distance: 4.4 mile loop

Time: 30 minuets to 1 hour

Highlights: Ridgetop ride, great singletrack and a variety of tread types, the fragrant pine forest around Pine swamp

Technical Difficulty: 1. Loads of great singletrack and doubletrack that are occasionally dotted with small rocks and roots. Some sandy trail sections might seem like the beach on this great ridge-top ride.

Aerobic Difficulty: Easy. This short ride has a small climb at the end and is a great introduction to some of the finest singletrack trail in southern Bald Eagle.

Vertical: 487 feet of climbing

Climbing Distance: 2.2 miles

Maps: DCNR Bald Eagle State Forest Public Use Map.

Land Status: DCNR Bald Eagle State Forest

39

Ride Notes: I truly can't invision a better mountain bike loop for budding mountain bikers than the Pine Swamp. This short but super-sweet loop is comprised of the things that mountain bikers dream about. Beginning at the Tower Trail, a flat grade cruises out along the top of Big Poe Mountain before embarking on an exhilarating descent to the Deep Low Place Trail. A carved turn in a fun mix of sand and loam soil follows more of the same out to Pine Swamp Road. A short section of forest road leads to the final fun challenge on the Plantation Trail. A potpourri of sand, grass and a few rocks makes every turn of the crank exciting. The final leg is a mellow climb on the smooth surface of Millheim Pike. You probably will find the loop to be stellar, that another-go-around may be in order!

THE RIDE...

0.0 From the trailhead pull-out with Mountain Church Road to your back, head straight into the woods on the singletrack Tower Trail, located just beyond the large boulders.

0.5 Cross a 4-way intersection with the Loggers Path.

1.5 Turn left at the T intersection on to Deep Low Place Trail.

1.9 Come out to the intersection of Pine Swamp Road and Poe Paddy Drive. Turn left on to Pine Swamp Road.

3.1 As Pine Swamp Road bends right, turn left (straight) on the Plantation Trail at a large set of boulders.

3.7 Pass a left-spur trail with a telephone line. Continue to follow the blue blazes on the trees.

3.9 Turn left on to Millheim Pike and climb back to the trailhead.

4.4 Trailhead.

Skull of the elusive and danger-ous "Hook-jaw knobbie-eater"

2 PINE SWAMP

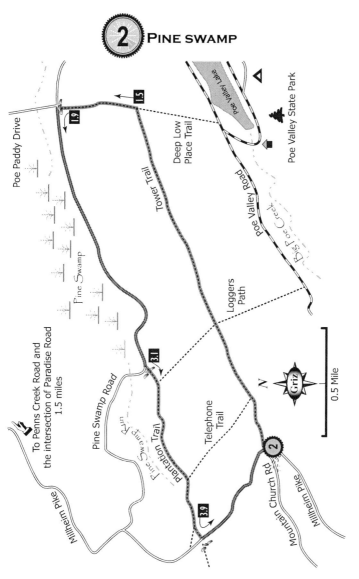

Poe Valley State Park

Poe Paddy Drive

Deep Low Place Trail

Poe Valley Lake

Poe Valley Road

Big Poe Creek

Tower Trail

Pine Swamp

Loggers Path

Pine Swamp Road

Pine Swamp Run

Plantation Trail

Telephone Trail

To Penns Creek Road and the intersection of Paradise Road 1.5 miles

Millheim Pike

Mountain Church Rd

Millheim Pike

N

Griz

0.5 Mile

1.5

1.9

3.1

3.9

BIG POE MOUNTAIN
RIDE 3

Trailhead: **Mountain Church and Millheim Pike Roads**, 23 miles from State College. From State College, travel east on U.S. 322 to Potters Mills. After passing Potters Mills, the highway will soon turn to a 4-lane expressway. Once on the expressway turn left at the second left turn, at the large brown sign stating 'Poe Valley State Park', on to Sand Mountain Road. Carefully follow this windy road 6 miles to a T intersection with Millheim Pike. Turn left on Millheim Pike and follow the road down the hill 1 mile. At the bottom of the hill, the road will become paved. Turn left at the fork on the gravel road, which is still Millheim Pike and climb the steep hill 1 mile. At the summit of the hill, Mountain Church Road will intersect with Millheim Pike. Park here in the large pull-out area on the right and the ride begins at this intersection. **GPS**: N40-49.11 W77-30.056'

Distance: 8.9 mile loop with an out and back section

Time: 1-3 hours

Highlights: Ridge top ride, great singletracks and a variety of tread types, the fragrant pine forest around Pine Swamp, Penns View the best view in Bald Eagle State Forest.

Technical Difficulty: 2+. Loads of great singletrack and doubletrack that are occasionally dotted with rocks and roots. Some sandy trail sections seem like the beach on this great ridge top ride. There is a super-short bike-hike on the Kerstetter Trail for riders that can't grind the Grade **4+** section.

Aerobic Difficulty: Easy to Moderate. This short ride does have a bit of climbing but over all its' a great introduction to some of the finest trail in southern Bald Eagle. The climbs are short and stout so enjoy the rewarding downhills.

Vertical: 1,099 feet of climbing

Climbing Distance: 4.4 miles

Maps: DCNR Bald Eagle State Forest Public Use Map.

Land Status: DCNR Bald Eagle State Forest

Ride Notes: This excellent short ride that runs around the Pine Swamp Flat atop Big Poe Mountain. The route covers moderate terrain with varied tread types and encounters some fun changes in elevation. The Pine Swamp is a beautiful ridge-top wetland situated near the summit knob of Big Poe Mountain. This fragrant forest is home to many critters including a few resident black bear. The ride begins an enjoyable journey out across the Tower Trail singletrack that becomes progressively more exciting with some mild rocky terrain. Carving a left on the Deep Low Place trail you become schooled in riding through sand and soft loamy soils as the ride leads to the Penns View. The view from here is arguably the best in all of Bald Eagle. From this precipitous perch you can see the towns of Coburn and Millheim as well as the Tunnel Mountain and the *Penns Creek Rail Trail (Ride #5)*. Retracing the road a bit

to the Kerstetter Trail, a daunting descent crosses Pine Swamp Run and climbs sharply to a forest road. More retraced road rolls to the next exciting section of wide singletrack that drops down a loose and bumpy trail. A sharp left turn has you reclimbing another steep before spinning out along Pine Swamp Road. The final section of wide, sandy singletrack cruises along the Plantation Trail leading to Millheim Pike and the trailhead.

THE RIDE...

0.0 From the trailhead pull-out with Mountain Church Road to your back, head straight into the woods on the singletrack Tower Trail, located just beyond the large boulders.

0.5 Cross a 4-way intersection with the Loggers Path.

1.5 Turn left at the T intersection on to Deep Low Place Trail.

1.9 Come out to the intersection of Pine Swamp Road and Poe Paddy Drive. Continue in a straight direction, riding on Poe Paddy Drive. As you travel on Poe Paddy make two (2) mental notes of trails. One trail is on the left at the sharp right bend around mile 2.4 and the second is the Kerstetter Trail on the right at mile 3.1.

3.6 Arrive at the impressive perch of Penns View. The Rail Trail you see below is part of the *Tunnel Mountain Trail and Penns Creek Rail Trail West (Rides 7 & 5)*. Retrace your way back to the Kerstetter Trail.

4.2 Turn left on the Kerstetter Trail at the trail sign.

4.6 Turn right on to Pine Swamp Road.

5.2 Turn right on to Poe Paddy Drive.

5.7 As Poe Paddy Drive bends right, turn hard left on the wide, unnamed (Musser Tr.?) grassy woods road blazed with blue blazes.

6.4 After a fun descent, turn hard left at the 4-way intersection, climbing back up the hill.

7.0 After passing a cabin on the left, follow the trail left as it comes out to Pine Swamp Road. Turn left on Pine Swamp Road (mile 7.2).

7.5 As Pine Swamp Road bends left, turn hard right on the Plantation Trail at a large set of boulders.

8.4 Turn left on to Millheim Pike and climb back to the trailhead.

8.9 Trailhead.

Panoramic Penns View

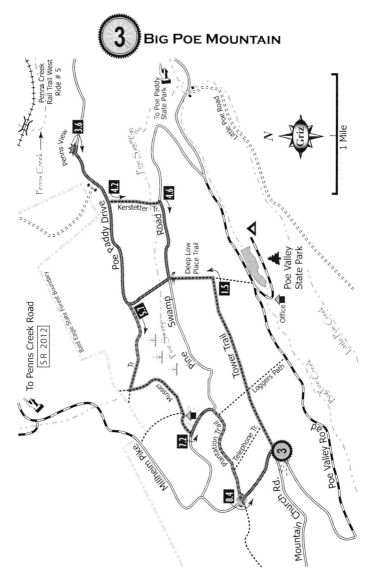

SEVEN MOUNTAINS ENDURO EPIC
RIDE 4

Trailhead: **Poe Valley State Park**, 25 miles from State College. From State College, travel east on U.S. 322 to Potters Mills. After passing Potters Mills, the highway will soon turn to a 4-lane expressway. Turn left at the second left turn on the expressway on to Sand Mountain Road, at the large brown sign stating 'Poe Valley State Park'. Carefully follow this windy road to a T intersection with Millheim Pike. Turn left on Millheim Pike and follow the road down the hill. At the bottom of the hill, the road will become paved. Follow the paved (Poe Valley Road) road 2.3 miles to Poe Valley State Park. Turn right into Poe Valley State Park and follow the park road up past the park office. Park anywhere in the lot, the ride begins at the park office. **GPS**: N40-49.195' W77-28.366'

Distance: 25.1 mile loop

Time: 4-7 hours

Highlights: A possible all-day ride of epic proportion, lots of climbing and descending, the most continuous sections of singletrack in the region, many technical sections, backcountry bog, awesome photo opportunities

Technical Difficulty: **4**. Panther Hollow Trail is a mile long section of brutal (Grade **5**) but rideable rocks. Designed by the CCC boys back in the day, this rugged trail is suited for those looking to test their mettle along this unforgiving and relentless section of terrain. The rest of the route varies in difficulty from fast, smooth sections of the Deep Low Place trail, bony ridge tops and the washed-out singletrack sections west of Millheim Pike.

Aerobic Difficulty: **Strenuous**. I've heard that this ride is 'tuff-e-nuff' on a dual-sport bike, let alone a mountain bike! Pedaling through the most continuous stretch of linked singletracks demands a lot of the rider not to mention the elevation gained throughout the route. Bring lots of extra food and water, you don't wanna bonk on this one!

4 SEVEN MOUNTAINS ENDURO EPIC

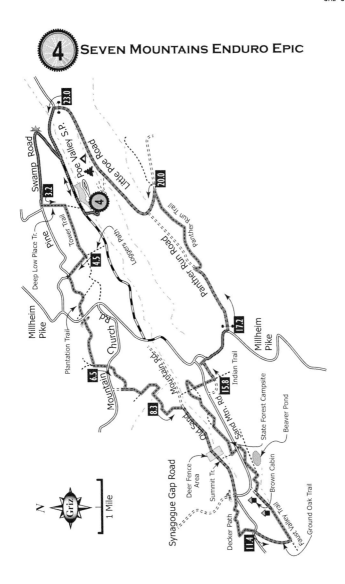

Southern Bald Eagle State Forest

Vertical: 3,653 feet of climbing
Climbing Distance: 13.3 miles
Maps: DCNR Bald Eagle State Forest Public Use Map.
Land Status: DCNR Bald Eagle State Forest
Ride Notes: Designed as a dual-sport dirt bike trail system by the Seven Mountains Ramblers, this loop is quite an outing. Covering loads of singletrack miles, crazy climbs and kamikaze descents, this route is truly a mountain riders' dream. For those who don't know, dual-sport bikes are basically street-legal motorcross bikes, built to run tough trail and highway all on the same steed. The route has been blazed with yellow blazes in one direction and due to the nature of the topography, it is best ridden backwards on a mountain bike. Check over your shoulder to catch a glimpse of these yellow blazes, to make sure you're on the right trail. This ride demands extra grub and water along with a good knowledge of bike handling and backcountary repair skills.

Beginning at the beautiful Poe Valley State Park, the ride warms up with a moderate climb on Pine Swamp Road. The Deep Low Place Trail dishes out the first round of sandy singletrack before climbing on to the Tower Trail. Dropping down off the ridge, the Plantation Trail begins a run across two forest roads and terminates on the Old Sand Mountain Road. Pull some tricks to get through the deer-fenced enclosure and coast along the road. The road ends at a unique junction and across the way a singletrack begins. The Decker Path rolls into the Ground Oak Trail, which ends at the Faust Valley Trail. Rumor has it that the remains of an old logging locomotive wreckage lie somewhere down in this hollow. The Faust Valley Trail turns woods road and links to yet another killer section of singletrack. Follow these turns carefully as they snake around the Sand Mountain ridge top. Climbing to the final burly challenge, the Panther Run Trail manages to suck riders onto its' rocky spine. After a mile and a half of brutal rock crawling, a screamer descent down Little Poe Road puts a goofy grin on your weary face. A mellow cruise leads back to Poe Valley Lake and the trailhead

THE RIDE...

0.0 From the park, head out to Poe Valley Road and turn right on Poe Valley Road.

1.4 Turn left on to Pine Swamp Road, climbing the dirt road. The trail passes a spectacular overlook vista at mile 1.9.

3.2 Turn left on to the wide singletrack of the Deep Low Place Trail. This turn is at the intersection of Pine Swamp and Poe Paddy Roads.

3.5 Turn right at the right spur on to the Tower Trail.

4.5 Turn right at the 4-way intersection, on to the Loggers Path and descend.

4.9 Turn left at a 4-way intersection at the base of the descent, on the sandy, wide old woods road. This is the Plantation Trail.

5.4 Pass a left spur trail under an old telephone line, and soon after pass a right spur woods road.

5.6 Keep left at a fork and cross Millheim Pike. The trail resumes on the other side of the road, between some large boulders. The trail winds down through fragrant white pines on some wicked-sick singletrack.

6.5 As the trail continues to climb on loose rock and sand, keep left at the fork as two lesser trails break right, leaving the State Forest lands. Soon after (mile 6.7) cross Mountain Church Road and continue on incredibly twisty singletrack. Pin those turns!

7.1 Turn left at the T intersection on to an old woods road.

7.9 The trail turns hard left (90 degrees). DO NOT turn right on the small obscure deer path. Soon after (mile 8.1), keep left at the fork and descend the steep, loose and sandy singletrack.

8.3 Cross the stream and choose either of the two lines that ascends the hill, they both rejoin higher up as they head left along the contour of the mountain. Soon after (mile 8.7) turn right on to Old Sand Mountain Road, a grassy woods road.

9.7 After passing through a deer-fence enclosure at the provided one-way swing-gates, pass a cabin and a spring on the left as the woods road widens.

10.4 At this interesting intersection of Sand Mountain, Synagogue Gap and Old Sand Mountain Roads, continue straight across Synagogue Gap Road and continue on a singletrack trail, the Decker Path, in the woods.

11.4 Cross Sand Mountain Road and descend the Ground Oak Trail 4-wheel drive road.

12.0 Turn left at the T intersection on to the Faust Valley Trail. Rumor has it that somewhere along this valley trail, lies the remains of an old iron logging locomotive.

13.1 Turn right on to the woods road, just opposite a driveway leading to a brown cabin. This is the second woods road on the right and if you arrive at Sand Mountain Road, you missed the turn. Immediately after turn left on to a wide singletrack that heads into a stand of pines. Check behind trees for the yellow blazes!

13.4 Cross a 4-way singletrack intersection above a beautiful backcountry beaver pond, check it out if you have time! Continue straight on the singletrack that runs parallel below Sand Mountain Road.

13.9 Cross Sand Mountain Road on to the Summit Trail, marked by the wooden sign. Once in the woods at the crest of the hill, turn right on to the right spur trail. DO NOT follow this trail and blue blazes straight down over the ridge. Soon after (mile 14.2), the trail comes out to a grassy woods road, passes a State Forest campsite and fire ring on the left. Approximately 50 feet before the grassy woods road merges with Sand Mountain Road, turn left on to the small and obscure singletrack.

14.7 Keep right at the fork, unless you want to visit a small vista via a sharp descent/ascent.

15.4 Keep left at a fork, dropping down a steep tram grade, cross the blue blazed Indian Trail and reascend the tram grade. Soon after (mile 15.7) the trail loops back and turns left on to the Indian trail, blazed blue. The Indian Trail will descend, crossing Sand Mountain Road. **You can bypass this tough section by staying right at the fork and then turning right on to the blue blazed Indian Trail.

15.8 Turn left at the T intersection on to the grassy woods road.

16.1 Merge right on to a gravel road and pass a cabin on the left. Soon after turn right on to Millhiem Pike and continue to climb.

17.2 Turn left on to the gated Panther Run Road.

18.4 Turn right on to the Panther Run Trail at a 4-way intersection. Soon after turn left at a left spur, continuing to follow the rocky Panther Hollow Trail.

Jay De-hay' droppin' in

20.0 Turn hard left on to Little Poe Road, the old woods road, at an overgrown vista. As you descend, keep right (mile 20.4) at the fork with Panther Run Road and run it out!

23.0 After passing around a gate, turn left on to Poe Valley Road.

25.1 Turn left into Poe Valley State Park to the trailhead.

"The earth is not ours...it does not belong to us. We belong to it."
Cheif Joseph, Nez Perce

PENNS CREEK RAIL TRAIL WEST
RIDE 5

Trailhead: Coburn, 2.5 miles from Millheim. From the intersection of State Highways 45 and 445 in the center of Millheim, follow Coburn Road 0.8 miles to State Road 2012. Merge right on State Road 2012 and follow it 1.7 miles to Coburn. In the village of Coburn, turn left on a paved road, crossing Penns Creek on an old green iron bridge. Once across the iron bridge, turn right into the huge lot with a feed mill and grainery. Park out of the way on the right, along the creek bank. **GPS**: N40-51.729' W77-27.848'

Distance: 7.8 miles out and back

Time: 1-2 hours

Highlights: Great family ride, one of the most scenic railroad grades in Pennsylvania, incredible fishing on Penns Creek, a classic old railroad tunnel, tailor the ride to any length you'd like.

Technical Difficulty: **0**. Probably the most technical aspect of the entire ride is allowing your eyes to adjust to the darkness in the old railroad tunnel. There are a bunch of large rocks that have fallen from the ceiling of the tunnel, so take care when riding through. Be aware that there is always a chance of rockfall from the ceiling above. The bridge across Penns Creek can be a challenge, as the boardwalk is just barely wide enough for some bike handlebars. Watch you don't hook your handlebars under the wooden railing and don't rub your body against the wood for fear of a nasty splinter.

Aerobic Difficulty: **Easy**. The ride follows a smooth, cinder-covered rail grade that changes little in elevation. The hardpacked surface drains well and provides a safe, stable and fast riding surface. A great ride for families, fishermen and new riders.

Vertical: 353 feet of climbing

Climbing Distance: 3.7 miles

Maps: DCNR Bald Eagle State Forest Public Use Map

Land Status: DCNR Bald Eagle State Forest

PENNS CREEK RAIL TRAIL WEST

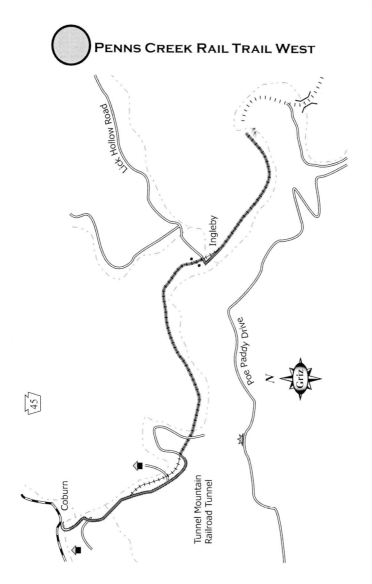

Lick Hollow Road

Ingleby

Poe Paddy Drive

N

Griz

45

Coburn

Tunnel Mountain
Railroad Tunnel

Ride Notes: What a short but fun ride for entry-level riders and young kids! The historic rail grade of the old Lewisburg & Tyronne Railroad is truly an outstanding ride for anyone who enjoys the magical combination of the two-wheels and woods. This well preserved rail-trail maintains its' original bed along with a handful of historical artifacts along the way. Built in the late 1800's the railway served to transport various goods from town to town, including lumber.

The ride begins at the feed mill in the quaint town of Coburn, just over the old green iron bridge across Penns Creek. The ride follows paved road which soon turns to dirt and parallels the creek. The current road strays from the original rail grade as it runs along the creek, right up to Tunnel Mountain where it takes an abrupt turn into the rocky hillside through the dank old railroad tunnel. Once on the other side, the grade crosses a tight wooden bridge built atop the original Lewisburg & Tyronne Railroad Bridge steel trusses and stone abutments. Across the bridge the ride continues a straight course as the meandering Penns Creek pulls away. An old mile-marker is spotted by the observant rider as the grade pulls into the small village of Ingleby and the Indian Rock. The classic "Indian Rock" stands as a modern meteorological marvel that has proved many weathermen wrong, see for yourself! The short sprint on the road will have you back on the rail-trail that leads to the terminus of the ride. At the turn-around point, the old bridge abutments stand like stone sentinels, painting a picture of this historic highway.

THE RIDE...

0.0 From the parking area, follow the rough-paved road as it runs southeast along Penns Creek.

1.1 As the road bends left, turn right into the old railroad tunnel and watch for large rocks on the floor of the tunnel. Once through the tunnel, cross a dirt road and a bridge over Penns Creek.

2.7 Pass through the village of Ingleby. Note the **Indian Weather**

Rock in the tripod, as crazy as it may be, there's a lot of truth to it all. The route follows the dirt road for a short way and will resume on the left as the old rail grade becomes apparent.

3.9 Come to the end of the trail at a rock abutment and large pile of broken concrete. The Rubble pile was originally the center abutment that helped support the span of the iron railroad bridge. There is another abutment on the opposite shore of Penns Creek where the railroad grade continues east. To ride this section, check out the *Penns Creek Rail Trail East (Ride # 7)* for directions and trail information. From this point, retrace the route back to the trailhead.

7.8 Trailhead.

What fills the mind of fanatic fly-fishermen...
The Green Drake

PENNS CREEK RAIL TRAIL EAST
RIDE 6

Trailhead: **Poe Paddy State Park**, 28 miles from State College. From State College, travel east on U.S. 322 to Potters Mills. After passing Potters Mills, the highway will soon turn to a 4-lane expressway. Turn at the second left turn on the expressway on to Sand Mountain Road, at the large brown sign stating 'Poe Valley State Park'. Carefully follow this windy road to a T intersection with Millheim Pike road. Turn left on Millheim Pike and follow the road down the hill. At the bottom of the hill, the road will become paved. Follow the paved (Poe Valley Road) road 5.7 miles, passing Poe Valley State Park, to Poe Paddy State Park Recreation Area. Turn left onto Poe Paddy Drive and once across the beautiful wooden span bridge, turn right into the parking area. The ride begins at the parking area by the wooden bridge. **GPS**: N40-50.063' W77-25.052'

Distance: 8.8 miles out and back

Time: 1 to 2 hours.

Highlights: Historic old railway, fun foot bridge built on original stone railroad abutments, interesting railroad tunnel, killer fishing on Penns Creek, Poe Paddy State Park amenities, remains of an old iron railroad bridge, tailor the ride to any length you'd like.

Technical Difficulty: **0**. Probably the most technical aspect of the entire ride is allowing your eyes to adjust to the darkness in the old railroad tunnel. Beware that there is always a chance of rockfall from the ceiling above. The bridge across Penns Creek can be a challenge, as the boardwalk is just barely wide enough for some bike handlebars. Watch you don't hook your handlebars under the wooden railing and don't rub your body against the wood for fear of a nasty splinter.

Aerobic Difficulty: **Easy**. The ride follows a smooth, cinder-covered rail grade that changes little in elevation. The hardpacked surface drains well and provides a safe, stable and fast riding surface. An excellent ride for families, fishermen and new riders.

Vertical: 460 feet of climbing

Climbing Distance: 4.1 miles

Maps: DCNR Bald Eagle State Forest Public Use Map.

Land Status: DCNR Bald Eagle State Forest

Ride Notes: An excellent fun ride for entry-level riders and young kids! The historic rail grade of the old Lewisburg & Tyronne Railroad is truly an outstanding ride for anyone who enjoys the magical combination of the two-wheels and woods. This well preserved rail-trail maintains the original bed along with a handful of historical artifacts along the way. Built in the late 1800's the railway served to transport various goods from town to town, including lumber.

The ride begins at the beautiful Poe Paddy State Park and follows the road grade out to the old bridge abutments that would have connected the old Lewisburg & Tyronne Railroad grade. If you have a chance to ride the *Penns Creek Rail Trail West (Ride #6),* you can visualize the connection of this great rail grade. Swinging back along the road which also happens to be the old railroad grade, the ride splits off left , following the grade out over Penns Creek. A tight wooden bridge built atop the original railroad bridge steel trusses and stone abutments, spans Penns Creek. The grade then takes a gentle turn into the rocky hillside and passes through the dank old railroad tunnel. A long stretch of cinder grade leads to a parking area where the rail trail turns to road. The final highlight is the old iron bridge above Cherry Run Road. From this point the ride returns back to the trailhead.

THE RIDE...

0.0 From the trailhead parking area, turn right on dirt road, following it out past some cabins.

1.1 Come to the stone abutments and a turn-around point. The rail trail continues on the opposite side of the creek from here and can be ridden on the *Penns Creek Rail Trail West* (Ride #6). Turn around and ride back down the grade as it turns back to dirt road.

1.6 Turn left on to the cinder old railroad grade, following it out across a **bridge** over Penns Creek and through a cool, wet old **railroad tunne**l.

3.9 The trail passes a parking area on the right and soon will merge with the road. Continue to follow the dirt road out.

Poe Paddy Tunnel

4.8 Turn left on to Cherry Run Road.

4.9 The ride ends at the old Lewisburg & Tyronne Railroad iron trestle bridge. From here retrace the route back to the trailhead.

8.8 Trailhead

The trestle over Penns Creek at Poe Paddy

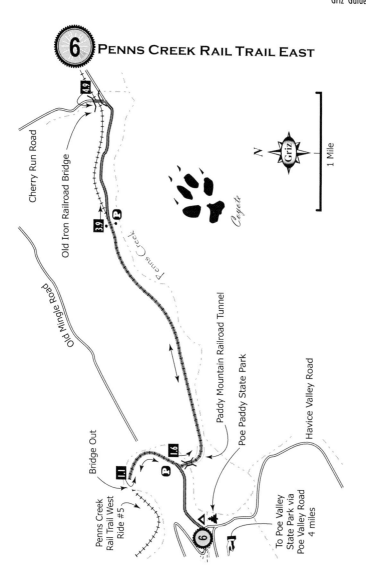

6 PENNS CREEK RAIL TRAIL EAST

N

Griz

1 Mile

Cherry Run Road

4.9

Old Iron Railroad Bridge

3.9

Penns Creek

Coyote

Old Mingle Road

Paddy Mountain Railroad Tunnel

Poe Paddy State Park

Havice Valley Road

Bridge Out

1.1

1.6

Penns Creek Rail Trail West Ride #5

6

To Poe Valley State Park via Poe Valley Road 4 miles

TUNNEL MOUNTAIN TRAIL
RIDE 7

Trailhead: **Poe Paddy State Park**, 28 miles from State College. From State College, travel east on U.S. 322 to Potters Mills. After passing Potters Mills, the highway will soon turn to a 4-lane expressway. Turn at the second left turn on the expressway on to Sand Mountain Road, at the large brown sign stating 'Poe Valley State Park'. Carefully follow this windy road to a T intersection with Millheim Pike road. Turn left on Millheim Pike and follow the road down the hill. At the bottom of the hill, the road will become paved. Follow the paved (Poe Valley Road) road 5.7 miles, passing Poe Valley State Park, to Poe Paddy State Park Recreation Area. Turn left onto Poe Paddy Drive and once across the beautiful wooden span bridge, turn right into the parking area. The ride begins at the parking area by the wooden bridge. **GPS**: N40-50.063' W77-25.052'

Distance: 21.8 mile loop

Time: 3-5 hours

Highlights: Best vistas in all of Bald Eagle State Forest, two historic railroad tunnels, historic railroad grade, lots of fast miles, world class trout stream fishing on Penns Creek, Poe Paddy and Poe Valley State Park amenities.

Technical Difficulty: 2+. Much of the ride covers mild terrain and tread. In a few places it gets a bit rough on three separate singletrack sections. The climb outta Millheim Pike, the descent off Poe Mountain and the link from Old Mingle Road to the Penns Valley Rail Trail are quite challenging with a Grade 5 rating.

Aerobic Difficulty: Strenuous. The ride rolls out through many miles and covers many climbs. The singletrack sections require some extra 'gas' to get through with challenging obstacles to break up the forest road and Rail Trail sections.

Vertical: 2,870 feet of climbing

Climbing Distance: 11.2 miles

Maps: DCNR Bald Eagle State Forest Public Use Map.
Land Status: DCNR Bald Eagle State Forest
Ride Notes: This excellent ride is taken from my second book *Mountain Biking Pennsylvania*. This revised version includes an improved digital map and mileage log produced with GPS software. The route contains two critical ride cruxes; one at mile 15.0 and the second at mile 20.0. Follow the directions carefully at these critical points to ensure you stay on route. The ride warms up with some great features like the first railroad bridge and tunnel as it rolls along the old Penns Creek Rail Trail. Passing under yet another historic railroad bridge, the ride climbs and then descends on some great forest road. A dead-end road marks the beginning of some serious off-camber singletrack along Penns Creek. Back on the Rail Trail, the ride passes over the second bridge and through the Tunnel Mountain tunnel, before spinning out a bunch of miles on the road. Climbing to the crux turn of the ride, a steep singletrack with tricky turns dumps you atop Poe Mountain, passing the spectacular Penns View overlook. Now for the Gums Trail finale, a short woods road climb to a downright dirty descent on the fall line. Super steep trail and loose tread prevail as you try n' fend off gravity's pull on this wicked drop. The next section is a bit cruxy as some creativity is needed to follow the trail out to Poe Valley Road where a short cool-down returns you to the trailhead.

THE RIDE...

0.0 From the trailhead turn right and cross the wooden bridge over Big Poe Creek. Follow the dirt road.
0.6 Turn hard right on the Penns Creek Rail Trail and follow the cinder grade on a bridge across Penns Creek. Shortly after you'll pass through the dank railroad tunnel.
2.8 Merge right on to the dirt road.
3.7 Turn left on Cherry Run Road and pass under the old iron railroad bridge.

5.0 Turn left, climbing Old Mingle Road.

8.1 After a great descent, turn right at the water's edge on the rough n' rocky singletrack that follows Penns Creek northwest.

8.7 Turn right on the Penns Creek Rail Trail at the large rock abutments.

9.8 Merge on to a dirt road and pass through the small village of Ingleby and the unique "Indian Weather Rock". Resume the ride on the cabled Penns Creek Rail Trail and soon after pass an old railroad mile-marker.

11.2 Cross a wooden footbridge built atop the old railroad bridge. If you look up to the south, you will see the open Penns View vista on Poe Paddy Drive. The ride climbs to this vista. Soon after pass through the Tunnel Mountain railroad tunnel.

12.3 Keep right as the road forks and becomes somewhat paved, following the creek.

12.5 Cross a green iron bridge into the village of Coburn. Once across the bridge, turn left on Penns Creek Road (aka State Road 2012).

14.1 Turn left on to a paved road that crosses Penns Creek and climbs. The road will soon merge left with Millheim Pike and continue to climb.

15.9 After passing the large wooden forestry sign welcoming you to the Bald Eagle State Forest and a vehicle pull-out on the left, turn left just past the telephone pole, climbing the steep, wide singletrack. This turn is the first crux.

16.3 After passing a right spur trail, turn left at the 4-way intersection on the Musser Trail, a wide ATV style trail.

16.9 Turn hard right at a 4-way intersection, continuing climbing the Musser Trail on a steep loose and rocky ATV style trail.

17.7 Turn left on Poe Paddy Drive.

19.0 Pass the incredible Penns View looking down on Tunnel Mountain.

19.4 Turn right on the Gums Trail old woods road. Soon the woods road will pass a right spur trail as it narrows down to a blue-blazed

7 Tunnel Mountain Trail

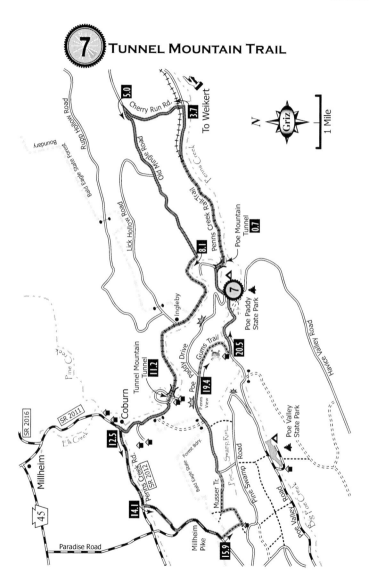

Cherry Run Rd. 5.0

To Weikert 3.7

Penns Creek

Old Mingle Road

Lick Hollow Road

Bald Eagle State Forest Boundary

Ruba Mofflin Road

N Griz

1 Mile

Poe Mountain Tunnel 0.7

Penns Creek Trail

8.1

Ingleby

7

Poe Paddy State Park

Tunnel Mountain Tunnel 11.2

Poe Paddy Drive

Penns View

Poe Gums Trail

20.5

19.4

Bald Eagle State Forest Bdry.

SR 2016

SR 2011

Coburn

12.5

Elk Creek

Millheim

45

Penns Creek Rd. SR 2012

14.1

Musser Tr.

Poe Swamp Run

Pine Swamp Road

Poe Valley State Park

Havice Valley Road

Big Poe Creek

Poe Valley Road

Millheim Pike

15.9

Paradise Road

singletrack trail.

20.5 After a harrowing descent, the trail becomes obscure. Follow the blue blazes as they lead down near Big Poe Creek and bear right, following the creek. This is the second crux! The trail will dump out on to a cabin driveway. Turn left on the driveway, cross the bridge and pass around the gate. Turn left on Poe Valley Road.

21.8 Turn left into Poe Paddy State Park to finish the ride at the trailhead.

Jay shreddin' the sand on the 'Enduro Epic'

BULL HOLLOW
RIDE 8

Trailhead: **Snyder-Middlewarth Natural and Picnic Area**, 32 miles from Lewisburg. From Lewisburg travel west on State Highway 45 to Laurelton Center and the junction of State Highway 235. Turn left on State Highway 235 following it south through the towns of Laurelton and Glen Iron. After cresting Penns Creek Mountain, turn right on to Hunter Road, your first right after cresting the hill. Hunter Road is a dirt forest road. Turn left on to Brieninger Gap Road and descend the hill to Swift Run Road. Turn right on Swift Run Road and follow it for 2 miles. Turn (fork) left staying on Swift Run Road and pass the Rock Springs Picnic Area. Turn right into the Snyder-Middlewarth Natural and Picnic Area. The ride begins from this parking area. **GPS**: N40-48.594' W77-16.908'

Distance: 13.6 mile loop

Time: 2-4 hours

Highlights: Snyder-Middleswarth and Tall Timbers Natural Areas and the Rock Springs and Snyder-Middleswarth Picnic Areas, great woodland ride on easy and well-maintained trail, excellent trail hiking at a pair of scenic natural areas.

Technical Difficulty: 1. The toughest part of the ride comes mid-loop when the route climbs a dirt road, which is a bit loose and stony, possibly rated at **3**. Most of the ride follows the smooth and hardpacked surface of forestry roads.

Aerobic Difficulty: Easy. The smooth fast tread throughout most of the route makes for a relatively easy pedal. The short section mid-ride climbs sharply and demands a bit more from the rider but is easily hiked by those who can't pedal it.

Vertical: 1,670 feet of climbing

Climbing Distance: 7.2 miles

Maps: DCNR Bald Eagle State Forest Public Use Map.

Land Status: DCNR Bald Eagle State Forest

Ride Notes: The perfect 'adventurous novice' ride, especially for those willing to spend a few hours pedaling through the wild woods of Pennsylvania. The ride has all the elements of a great intermediate mountain bike loop without the technical suffering and long miles. The trailhead location is a post-card scene in itself. The combination of the Snyder-Middleswarth and Tall Timbers natural areas makes for a great side-trip outing while visiting the area. Over 1,050 acres of old growth forest awaits your hiking curiosity. The closest tract to the trailhead is the 500-acre Snyder-Middleswarth Natural Area filled with massive old-growth pines and hemlocks. Hiking up through this enchanting forest, trails lead into the western tract of the 660-acre Tall Timbers Natural Area cloaked in second-growth oaks, pines and hemlocks.

Beginning at the beautiful Snyder-Middleswarth Natural and Picnic Area, the ride begins its journey through the forest passing the impressive rock slab and escarpment of the Rock Springs Picnic Area. This unique geologic feature is worth exploring after the ride. Bull Hollow Road is the turning point as the ride follows this changing road from well-maintained dirt to more of a 4-wheel drive trail. Many cabins are passed along the way as the trail slowly climbs up through the hollow to the mid-point of the ride. A switchback in the Bull Hollow Trail ascends an abrupt hill, crossing Little Mountain and rolls out to Hunter Road. From here the ride ducks back in on an unnamed gated wood road before exiting on Short Mountain Road and retracing the route back to the trailhead. Don't forget to stop by and check out the Rock Springs formation. If ya' have some extra time, its 'mucho recomendo' to take a hike through the Tall Timbers and Snyder-Middleswarth Natural Areas.

THE RIDE...

0.0 From the trailhead, ride out to Swift Run Road and turn left.
0.9 Turn left on to Short Mountain Road.
1.4 Turn left on to Bull Hollow Road.
4.1 Bull Hollow Road turns to Bull Hollow Trail as the road

8 BULL HOLLOW

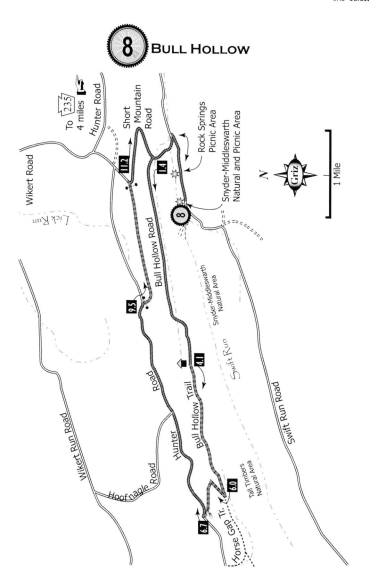

becomes grassy, more narrow and unmaintained.

6.0 Turn hard right on the woods roads as it climbs over Little Mountain.

6.7 After passing around the large boulders, turn right on to Hunter Road.

9.5 Turn right on to the unnamed gated woods road.

11.2 Pass around a gate and turn right on to Short Mountain Road.

12.3 Pass Bull Hollow Road on the right, continue on Short Mountain Road.

12.7 Turn right on to Swift Run Road.

13.7 Turn right into the trailhead lot at Snyder-Middleswarth State Park Natural Area.

STRONG MOUNTAIN SURPRISE
RIDE 9

Trailhead: **Penns Mountain ATV/Snowmobile trailhead parking area**, 26 miles from Lewisburg. From Lewisburg travel west on State Highway 45 to Laurelton Center and the junction of State Highway 235. Turn left on State Highway 235 following it south through the towns of Laurelton and Glen Iron. At the crest of Penns Creek Mountain, turn right into the large gravel ATV/Snowmobile trailhead parking area. The ride begins in the far right (northwest) corner of the lot. **GPS**: N40-50.116' W77-11.561'

Distance: 33.1 mile loop

Time: 6-9 hours

Highlights: Old log chute 'surprise' descent, loads of miles, lots of climbing, great woodland vistas, Snyder-Middleswarth and Rock Springs Natural and Picnic Areas, all-day adventure of epic proportions.

Technical Difficulty: **3+**. The ride has it's fun spots of singletrack, doubletrack and an awesome old log chute descent which is quite hairy (rated **5+**). Although the ride may be long, it isn't ultra-technical so it goes a bit faster than more technical routes.

Aerobic Difficulty: **Moderate to Strenuous**. A fun long-haul is a good way to describe the ride. Lots of ups and downs with fast sections of forest roads to link it all together. Make no mistake that with 33 off-road miles and almost 5,000 feet of climbing, there are lots of miles to cover in a day so go prepared for a good burn!

Vertical: 4,862 feet of climbing

Climbing Distance: 18.0 miles

Land Status: DCNR Bald Eagle State Forest

Maps: DCNR Bald Eagle State Forest Public Use Map.

Ride Notes: Epic could be a good way to describe the ride, especially if you're not fully prepared. The miles are not technically grueling nor are the climbs so venomously vertical, but to complete this ride in style get an early start, have lots of food and water and a bail-out plan if a mechanical should arise. The Strong Mountain Surprise is a great tour of the southeastern section of Bald Eagle State Forest. You will put in a fair amount of miles on forestry roads but this ride is far from a 'roady' spin through the forest. Numerous singletracks and doubletracks become the mainstay of the route, with many hidden surprises along the way.

The ride begins on the far reaches of the southeastern section of Bald Eagle and soon jumps on the great rolling singletrack of the Middle Ridge Trail. Forestry road links the next singletrack section along the old tram grade of the Cold Spring Trail. More forestry road cruises out Bull Hollow, gradually morphing from well-maintained forest road to 4-wheel drive road and finally singletrack. The singletrack slides into Horse Gap and grunts out of Greene Gap to pass a set of vistas on both faces of Thick Mountain at the mid-point of the ride. Howling up through Wolf Gap the ride passes yet another vista before droppin' in on the Pine Ridge Trail. Passing under Short Knob, the ride takes another stout climb up and over 'Hightop' point on Jacks Mountain and drops down the crux of the ride, an obscure wicked-steep old log chute. The chute drops a full 1,200 feet in a mere half mile and the descent can be downright dangerous! Forest roads climb back towards the Middle Ridge Trail that is gained via the Henstep Gap Trail, and retraces the ride back to the trailhead.

THE RIDE...

0.0 With State Highway 235 to your back, enter the ATV trail in the upper right corner of the lot. Soon after, turn right at the T intersection.

0.6 Exit the woods at the intersection of Henstep Valley Road (gravel woods road) and State Highway 235. Turn left on Henstep Valley Road Trail. Soon after (mile 0.8) keep left at the fork, staying on the ungated woods road.

1.3 Bear left at the fork, staying on the Henstep Valley Road Trail. At this point the trail becomes a 4-wheel drive road.

2.5 Turn left on to the wide singletrack of the Summit Trail, marked by the blue blazes. Soon after (mile 2.7), at the crest of the ridge, turn right at the 4-way intersection on to the Middle Ridge Trail.

3.7 Cross a 4-way intersection with the Henstep Gap Trail (Not Henstep Valley Road Trail), and soon after (mile 4.0) pass a large rock outcrop on the right.

5.3 After a sweet descent, turn left on Henstep Valley Road Trail 4-wheel drive road.

5.5 Turn left on to Hunter Road. At mile 6.5 pass Sand Spring on the right.

7.2 Turn right on to Brieninger Gap Road and approximately 100 yards, turn right on to the wide, grassy Cold Spring Trail. Soon after (mile 7.6) keep left at the fork.

9.0 Turn left at the T intersection on Short Mountain Road. At the bottom of the hill (mile 9.3) turn right on to the dirt road, Bull Hollow Road. After passing a cabin (mile 12.1), the road becomes a narrow 4-wheel drive road.

13.9 Continue straight on the Horse Gap Trail singletrack as a rocky woods road breaks off and switchbacks.

9 STRONG MOUNTAIN SURPRISE

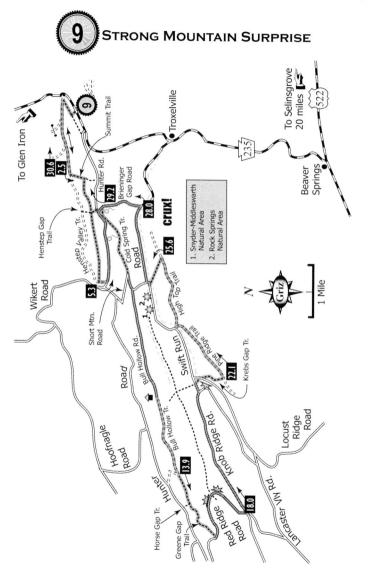

14.8 Turn left over the slick wooden bridge in Horse Gap, and once across turn left again, ascending the Greene Gap Trail.

15.9 Turn left on to Red Ridge Road.

16.7 Pass a nice view on the left and soon after pass the Thick Mountain and High Top Trails at the ridge top (mile 16.9).

18.0 Turn left at the 4-way intersection on Knob Ridge Road. Along this long stretch you'll pass the Krebs Gap Trail (mile 19.7) and Old Lancaster Valley Road (mile 21.0).

21.3 Turn right at the large boulders, onto the yellow blazed, wide grassy singletrack. Soon after (mile 21.5) cross Locust Ridge Road diagonally left, continuing on the marked singletrack of the Krebs Gap Trail. The trail also passes the New Lancaster Valley vista at the road crossing.

22.1 Turn left on the old woods road, Pine Ridge Trail.

23.9 Turn right at the fork on the 4-wd road, High Top Trail.

25.6 After cresting the High Top Mountain summit (mile 25.1) turn left on a singletrack at the faded, yellow blazed (with double bands) on a large oak tree. This turn is approximately 0.5 miles down from the summit and obscure! The trail bends back left into thicker woods and descends a sick straight line down a rocky old log slide. Buckle up! Its gonna get burly!

26.1 Jump across the small creek and turn right on to Swift Run Road. Soon after (mile 26.2) turn right at the T intersection continuing on Swift Run Road.

28.0 Turn left on Brieninger Gap Road and climb.

29.2 Cross Hunter Road at the T intersection and climb the Henstep Gap Trail, marked at the wooden trail sign. Soon after (mile 29.4) turn right at the 4-way intersection of the Middle Ridge Trail.

30.5 Turn left, descending the Summit Trail and merge right on to the gravel Henstep Valley Road, retracing the route back to the trailhead.

32.7 Turn right on to the ATV trail at the intersection of Henstep Valley Road and State Highway 235

33.1 Turn left at the left-spur and finish at the trailhead.

MIDDLE RIDGE TO HENSTEP VALLEY
RIDE 10

Trailhead: **Penns Mountain ATV/Snowmobile trailhead parking area**, 26 miles from Lewisburg. From Lewisburg travel west on State Highway 45 to Laurelton Center and the junction of State Highway 235. Turn left on State Highway 235 following it south through the towns of Laurelton and Glen Iron. At the crest of Penns Creek Mountain, turn right into the large gravel ATV/Snowmobile trailhead parking area. The ride begins in the far right (northwest) corner of the lot. **GPS**: N40-50.116' W77-11.561'

Distance: 10.5 mile loop

Time: 1-3 hours

Highlights: Outstanding singletrack trail with a challenging 4-wheel drive road, great woodland scenery, options to link this ride with *Penns Creek Mountain or Booney Mountain, Rides #11 and/or #12* from the same trailhead.

Technical Difficulty: 2. The Middle Ridge singletrack offers some great terrain, from smooth and silky to rooted and bumpy. The Henstep Valley Trail is a wild combination of 4-wheel drive road and freshly graded logging road. This route runs the gamut from rocks and roots to smooth hardpacked sections.

Aerobic Level: Easy to Moderate. The ride is rolling in nature with short climbs and descents. The bumpy terrain requires a bit of cranking in more technical sections.

Vertical: 1,380 feet of climbing

Climbing Distance: 4.7 miles

Maps: DCNR Bald Eagle State Forest Public Use Map.

Land Status: DCNR Bald Eagle State Forest

Ride Notes: An awesome singletrack is the lead out and a rugged 4-wheel road as the return. This ride offers some varied terrain for the adventurous novice or seasoned pro riders. Right from the trailhead the ride ducks into the dense forest on ATV trail. Connecting with Henstep Valley Road, the ride climbs to the Middle Ridge Trail.

This great singletrack runs atop the ridge, passing unique rock formations on excellent trail. A snappy descent turns back on the Henstep Valley Road, which rambles back to the trailhead. A great all-around ride that highlights an outstanding singletrack. If you feel energetic enough, link this ride with *Ride #11, Penns Creek Mountain* or the more commiting *Ride #12, Booney Mountain*.

THE RIDE...

0.0 With State Highway 235 to your back, enter the ATV trail in the upper right corner of the lot. Soon after, turn right at the T intersection.

0.5 Exit the woods at the intersection of Henstep Valley Road (gravel woods road) and State Highway 235. Turn left on to Henstep Valley Road. Soon after (mile 0.8) keep left at the fork, staying on the ungated woods road.

1.3 Bear left at the fork, staying on the Henstep Valley Road. At this point the trail becomes a 4-wheel drive road.

2.5 Turn left on to the wide singletrack of the Summit Trail, marked by the blue blazes. Soon after (mile 2.8), at the crest of the ridge, turn right at the 4-way intersection on to the Middle Ridge Trail.

3.8 Cross a 4-way intersection with the Henstep Gap Trail (Not Henstep Valley Road). Soon after (mile 4.3) pass a large rock outcrop on the right.

5.3 After a sweet descent, turn right on Henstep Valley Road 4-wheel drive road and retrace your route back to the trailhead.

8.1 Pass the Summit Trail on the right.

9.7 Bear right as the Henstep Valley Road heads out to State Highway 235.

10.0 Turn right on to the ATV trail and follow it back to the trailhead.

10.5 Turn left at the left-spur ATV trail and finish at the trailhead.

10 MIDDLE RIDGE TO HENSTEP VALLEY

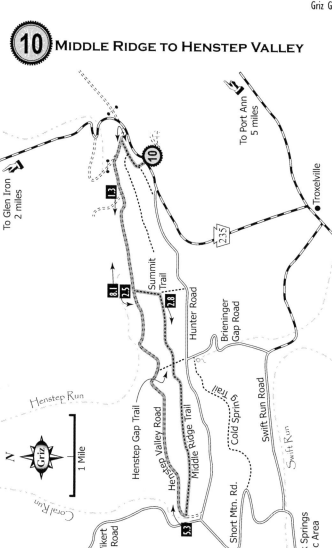

To Glen Iron
2 miles

To Port Ann
5 miles

Troxelville

235

Summit Trail

Hunter Road

Brieninger Gap Road

Cold Spring Trail

Swift Run Road

Henstep Run

Middle Ridge Trail

Henstep Valley Road

Henstep Gap Trail

Coral Run

Wikert Road

Short Mtn. Rd.

Swift Run

Rock Springs Picnic Area

N
Griz

1 Mile

75

PENNS CREEK MOUNTAIN
RIDE 11

Trailhead: **Penns Mountain ATV/Snowmobile trailhead parking area**, 26 miles from Lewisburg. From Lewisburg travel west on State Highway 45 to Laurelton Center and the junction of State Highway 235. Turn left on State Highway 235 following it south through the towns of Laurelton and Glen Iron. At the crest of Penns Creek Mountain, turn right into the large gravel ATV/Snowmobile trailhead parking area. The ride begins in the far right (northwest) corner of the lot. **GPS**: N40-50.116' W77-11.561'

Distance: 8.2 mile loop

Time: 1-2 hours

Highlights: Outstanding ATV trail with a challenging 4-wheel drive road, great woodland scenery, options to link this ride with *Rides #10 and/or #12* from the same trailhead.

Technical Difficulty: 2. The most technical section comes about mid-ride with a descent off the 2,100 foot summit knob of Penns Creek Mountain. This old woods road is somewhat steep, loose and rocky. Carefully picking your way down this old road should be a fun challenge and may raise the technical difficulty to a **3+**.

Aerobic Level: Easy to Moderate. The ride initially follows an easy grade in but climbs more steeply to the summit of Penns Creek Mountain. The descent is mostly downhill as it rolls back to the trailhead.

Vertical: 1,417 feet of climbing

Climbing Distance: 4.2 miles

Maps: DCNR Bald Eagle State Forest Public Use Map.

Land Status: DCNR Bald Eagle State Forest

Ride Notes: The Penns Creek Mountain is a great alternative to *Booney Mountain (Ride #12)* because it cuts out the real committing steep and technical section deep in Moyer Gap. The ride runs the short loop designated for ATV use in the Bald Eagle State Forest and makes for a fun and challenging ride. Starting at the trailhead lot on the west side of State Highway 235, the ride follows the highway north before crossing to the east side. Narrow trail gives way to wider old forest road as the ride begins a slow climb. Passing the exit trail, the grade gets steeper and passes an old overgrown vista on the right. At the apex of the mountain a series of trails worth exploring awaits the curious rider but those following the route will begin a steep descent on

What do you see?

a degraded logging road. Looping around the south face of Penns Creek Mountain the ride rejoins East Kettle Road and rolls back to the trailhead.

THE RIDE...

0.0 With State Highway 235 to your back, enter the ATV trail in the upper right corner of the lot. Soon after, turn right at the T intersection.

0.5 Exit the woods at the intersection of Henstep Valley Road (gravel woods road) and State Highway 235. Carefully cross and State Highway 235 and resume the yellow blazed ATV trail on the opposite side of the highway. Once in the woods, keep left at the fork and ride out to East Kettle Road, just behind a gate. Turn right on East Kettle Road (mile 0.7) and begin a slow climb.

2.6 Pass a right-spur woods road. This road is the exit of your loop.

4.0 After passing the overgrown vista on the right (mile 3.7), come to the small circle turn-around atop Penns Creek Mountain. At the top right end, turn on to the ATV trail that begins to descend. Soon after, keep right at the fork.

5.1 Keep straight (right) as a trail switchbacks left and descends.

5.7 Turn left at the T intersection on East Kettle Road.

7.7 Turn left before the gate and follow the ATV trail back across State Highway 235. Retrace the ATV trail back to the trailhead.

8.2 Turn left at the left-spur and follow it out to the trailhead.

11 PENNS CREEK MOUNTAIN

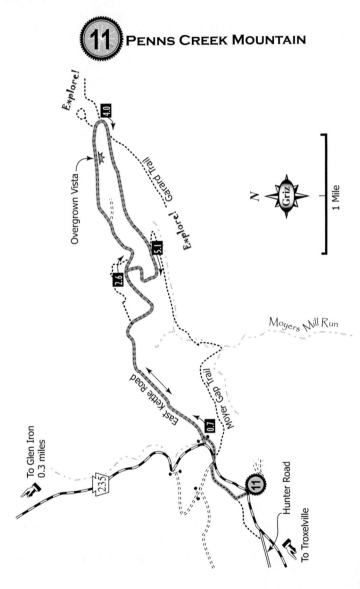

Explore!

4.0

Overgrown Vista

Garard Trail

Explore!

5.1

2.6

Moyers Mill Run

N Griz

1 Mile

East Kettle Road

Moyer Gap Trail

0.7

To Glen Iron
0.3 miles

235

11

Hunter Road

To Troxelville

BOONEY MOUNTAIN
RIDE 12

Trailhead: **Penns Mountain ATV/Snowmobile trailhead parking area**, 26 miles from Lewisburg. From Lewisburg travel west on State Highway 45 to Laurelton Center and the junction of State Highway 235. Turn left on State Highway 235 following it south through the towns of Laurelton and Glen Iron. At the crest of Penns Creek Mountain, turn right into the large gravel ATV/Snowmobile trailhead parking area. The ride begins in the far right (northwest) corner of the lot. **GPS**: N40-50.116' W77-11.561'

Distance: 7.8 mile loop

Time: 1-3 hours

Highlights: Stream crossings, remote trail in a dark, dank and deep gap, steep climbs and descents, burly technical trail, old tram trail, can be linked with *Rides #10 and/or #11*.

Technical Difficulty: **4**. The upper part of the ride runs the ridge on moderately rocky trail and old woods road. The descent off the south face of Penns Creek Mountain steps up the challenge and the final leg through the dank Moyer Gap is downright burly. Be prepared for large loose rocks, slick roots, stream crossings, mud holes and a few stout logs.

Aerobic Difficulty: **Moderate to Strenuous**. This sustained ride begins with a cruise out across the mountain top ridge that'll get the heart going. A smoking singletrack then leads to the final climb out of Moyer Gap. Sustained and somewhat steep, the old tram trail follows a consistent grade back to the ridge top on mixed ground.

Vertical: 1,547 feet of climbing

Climbing Distance: 4.0 miles

Maps: DCNR Bald Eagle State Forest Public Use Map.

Land Status: DCNR Bald Eagle State Forest

Ride Notes: Originally designed by loggers and currently designated as an ATV area, Booney Mountain holds a little known secret amongst it's flanks. Buried deep in the bowels of Moyer Gap lies some of the sketchiest singletrack and technical riding around. "Steep n' Deep" is one of many ways to describe the overall route but you may find yourself using words like 'Burly' or 'Bad-ass'!

Beginning with a mellow but sustained climb, the trail crosses the highway and wanders along East Kettle Road, a dirt forest road. Splitting off up into the woods is a short section of technical and off-camber ATV riding through dense saplings and hardwoods. Back on the forest road, things get rockier with elevation, where the trail hooks sharp right and drops off the steep south face into the Moyer Gap abyss. Steep and progressively more rocky is what you'll experience as the sun becomes shut out by the ancient hemlocks above. Dankness coats the trail and all the uneven obstacles along the way, as gravity and grace become your Yin and Yang. Stream-hopping and mud pits prevail all the way down to the crux turn onto the old tram trail.

Once you find the crux yellow blazed trail, it's a long ride out on some of the finest preserved tram trail in this region. Off-camber and 8 inches wide at first, the trail eventually widens out a bit but still tosses you a few technical rock gardens. The top-out is 'oh-so-sweet' as you pedal back to the trailhead thinking of how you may have nearly cheated death in the hellhole of Moyer Gap. Link this ride with the *Strong Mountain Surprise (Ride #9)* trail for a stellar hardman, all-day outing!

THE RIDE...

0.0 With State Highway 235 to your back, enter the ATV trail in the upper right corner of the lot. Soon after, turn right at the T intersection.

0.5 Exit the woods at the intersection of Henstep Valley Road (gravel woods road) and State Highway 235. Carefully cross and State Highway 235 and resume the yellow blazed ATV trail on the opposite side of the highway. Once in the woods, keep left at the

12 BOONEY MOUNTAIN

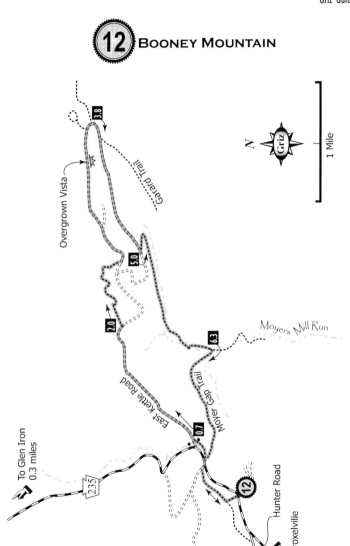

fork (the right fork is your exit trail) and ride out to East Kettle Road, just behind a gate. Turn right on East Kettle Road (mile 0.7) and begin a slow climb.

2.0 Turn left up the wide ATV trail that winds up into the woods.

2.9 Merge left onto East Kettle Road.

3.6 Pass an old, overgrown vista on the right.

3.9 Come to a small circle turn-around. At the top right end, turn on to the ATV trail that begins to descend. Soon after, keep right at the fork.

5.1 Turn hard left at the switchback (left spur). Follow the progressively rocky trail carefully down into the bowels of the Moyers Mill Run drainage. Enjoy the spooky, dank atmosphere created by the ancient, looming hemlocks and the heinously rocky terrain ahead. Watch for slick rocks and roots in this wet, mossy drainage. (*Note: This is your last chance to bail, going straight will bring you out on to East Kettle Road.)

6.3 Turn hard (120 degrees) right on to a yellow blazed singletrack, climbing this incredible old tram grade. The blazes are faint and the trail is initially obscure, so <u>look keenly for this crux move</u>!

7.2 Turn left at the T intersection on to the ATV trail and carefully cross State Highway 235. Continue on the ATV trail as it ducks back into the woods at the intersection of Henstep Valley Road and State Highway 235.

7.8 Turn left at the left-spur trail to finish up at the trailhead lot.

L: The crux turn out of Moyer Gap on the old logging grade

R: ATV riders down in the 'Gap'

SHADE MOUNTAIN
RIDE 13

Trailhead: **Shade Mountain ATV/Snowmobile trailhead parking area**, 25 miles from Selinsgrove. From Selinsgrove travel west on U.S. 522 to Beaver Springs. After passing through Beaver Springs, turn left on State Highway 235, traveling south for 4 miles. At the crest of Shade Mountain turn right into the large gravel parking area on the left, marked by a large wooden forestry sign. The ride begins mid-lot on a singletrack trail. **GPS**: N40-41.756' W77-15.600'

Distance: 12.9 mile loop

Time: 2-4 hours

Highlights: Technical motocross-style singletrack, miles of rugged trail, ridgetop ride, lots of bail-out points.

Technical Difficulty: 3+. The ride follows a motorcross network of trail so it will contain obstacles meant to challenge motorcross bikes. Loose rock and washed-out trail sections are a given. Short but moderate rock gardens are found throughout the ride with the exception of the end of the ride where a longer stretch (rated **4+**) is traversed. Some logs are down but skilled riders will chew right through them. Finally the climbs and descents require some care by all riders with the loose and unstable nature of the trail.

Aerobic Difficulty: Moderate. Due the undulating nature of the ride, it demands that you constantly 'shift the clutch' and 'stay on the gas'. The terrain lays down a few fun, but challenging obstacles, making you work hard from section to section. Not terribly difficult but definitely not to be taken lightly.

Vertical: 2,695 feet of climbing

Climbing Distance: 6.7 miles

Maps: DCNR Bald Eagle State Forest Public Use Map.

Land Status: DCNR Bald Eagle State Forest

Ride Notes: Shade Mountain is the only place in Pennsylvania State Forests that you can legally ride a motorcross bike (with approved spark arrestor!). This hidden gem for dirt bikers has proved to be a formidable challenge for mountain bikes. After all, a mountain bike is pretty much a dirt bike minus some cool sound effects and a motor! In this ridge-top trail system you will find all trails are blazed yellow in both directions. Since the trail is blazed in both directions, one would assume that this is a two-way trail, so watch for motorcross bikes from both directions. Designed as a motorcross trail, the ride covers challenging terrain in sections as it straddles the north and south faces of Shade Mountain. Rock gardens, tight and twisty singletrack are just some of the technical teasers you'll encounter. There are also many snappy turns and side trails, so keep alert to stay on route!

Dividing the ridge-top is Shade Mountain Road, a forest access road. Working from the south and crossing to the north side of the ridge, the trail jumps right into stellar sections of trail. Flat, mossy, wide singletrack leads to tight, twisty woods runs. A few short descents and climbs will once again cross the Shade Mountain Road. If you thought the first half was a blast, get ready for more! A bunch of sweet drops with some fine singletrack winds westward along the south flank of the ridge. The final bone comes in the last two miles with rocky challenges and some tricky singletrack. Slide across the small wooden bridge and finish up with a mellow climb back to the trailhead.

THE RIDE...

0.0 With State Highway 235 to your back and facing the woods, there are three trails that leave from the parking area; one at each corner and one in the middle. The left corner is an old woods road, do not take that trail. The right corner is a singletrack, which will be where the ride exits from. Begin the ride on the singletrack that is just a bit left of the middle of the trailhead lot.

0.4 Cross a small wooden bridge and soon after pass a 4-way intersection.

2.2 Turn left at the T intersection, cross Shade Mountain Road and

Day Dreaming...

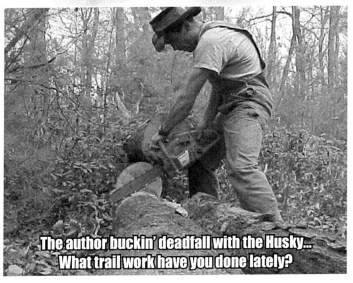

The author buckin' deadfall with the Husky...
What trail work have you done lately?

continue on the Diamond Trail marked by the wooden sign.

2.5 Turn right at the T intersection. Soon after (30 yards) keep straight at the left-spuring trail, staying on the wide singletrack.

3.1 Pass a 4-way intersection, continue straight. Soon after (0.1 mile) you'll pass a radio tower on the left as the trail turns to a gravel road.

3.3 Turn left at the T intersection (actually a faint trail heads straight so I guess it could be a 4-way intersection) on to the Mitchell Trail grassy old woods road. Ride for approximately 300 yards and look carefully on the right for an obscure right turn on a singletrack trail, turn right on to this singletrack. This trail is found just before the woods road passes over a small rock garden. This is the crux of the entire ride!

4.2 Turn right at the T intersection climbing the wide, rocky, Tram Trail. Soon after (mile 4.4), turn left on to the singletrack trail.

5.3 Turn right at the T intersection on to the Shawverville Trail, climbing the wide old woods road. Soon after (mile 5.5) cross Shade Mountain Road and descend the steep hill. The trail will turn hard right at the bottom of the hill (mile 5.7).

6.5 Turn left at the 4-way intersection, just before the Tram Trail.

7.9 Keep left at the fork.

8.3 As the singletrack becomes a wide, grassy woods road (Mitchell Path), turn left onto the obscure singletrack. Soon you will pass under a vista at a small clear-cut. Soon after the trail bends left as another trail merges in from the right, descending.

8.6 The trail bends hard right at the white blazed trees, (State Forest boundary markers). Soon after the trail almost comes out on to Shade Mountain Road, stay in the woods on the singletrack.

10.2 Continue straight at the right-spur trail (Diamond Trail), riding the rockier terrain ahead.

11.5 Pass the Cobble Path on the left, marked by the small wooden sign.

12.0 Cross the small wooden bridge over Lost Creek.

12.9 Leave the woods into the trailhead parking lot.

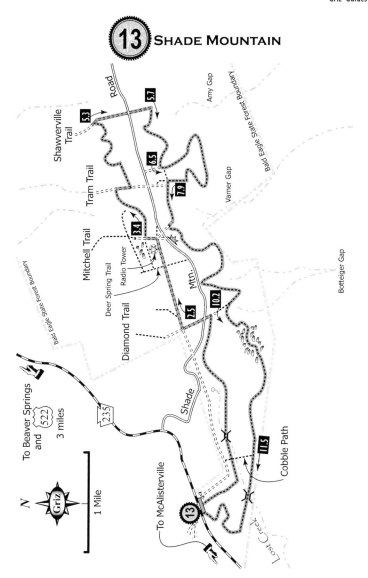

13 SHADE MOUNTAIN

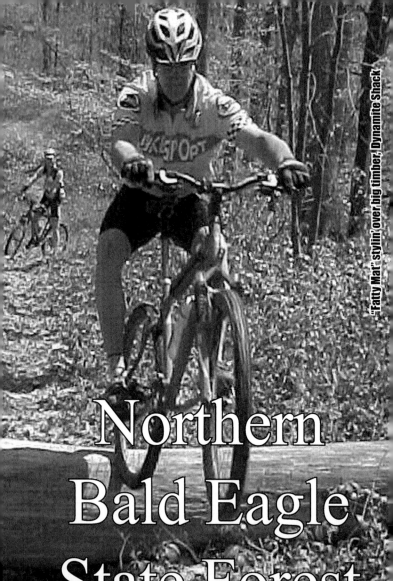

"Fatty Mat" stylin' over big timber, Dynamite Shack

Northern
Bald Eagle
State Forest

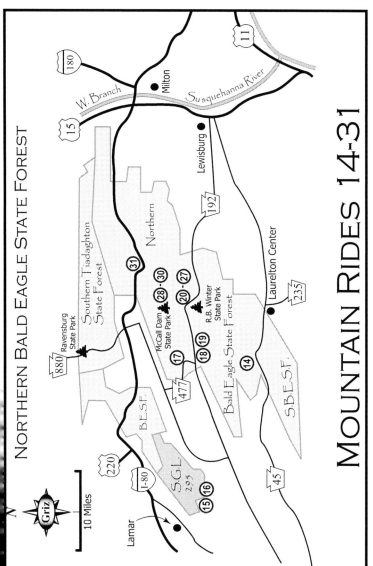

ROUND TOP MOUNTAIN LOOKOUT
RIDE 14

Trailhead: **Winklebleck and Stony Run Roads**, 22 miles from Lewisburg. From Lewisburg travel west on State Highway 45. Four miles past Laurelton Center and the junction of State Highway 235, turn right on to Winklebleck Road just past the Hairy Johns Picnic Area. Bear (turn) right at the T intersection with Round Top Road, staying on Winklebleck Road. Come to a T intersection with Stony Run Road, park on the wide shoulder near the intersection along either road. The ride begins at the intersection. **GPS**: N40-55.470' W77-17.220'

Time: 30 minuets to 1 hour

Distance: 5.5 mile loop

Highlights: Incredible vista overlooking the beautiful Penns Valley, historic signal tower, smooth and well-maintained trail.

Technical Difficulty: 1. The ride follows well-maintained forestry roads and old woods roads carpeted with grass. These roads do have a few fun obstacles along the way, all of which can be avoided. An excellent ride for bikers of all abilities!

Aerobic Difficulty: Easy. The ride follows a smooth grade both up and down the mountain, making for an easy cruise. The smooth and hardpacked nature of the forestry roads keep your tires rolling along as you take in the scenery of this great ride.

Vertical: 720 feet of climbing

Climbing Distance: 2.8 miles

Maps: DCNR Bald Eagle State Forest Public Use Map.

Land Status: DCNR Bald Eagle State Forest

Ride Notes: Don't let the mellow climb intimidate you outta riding this loop. A spectacular summit awaits the lucky folks willing to pedal this loop and the climb is much easier than it appears on paper. Beginning at the intersections of Stony Run and Winklebleck Roads, the ride begins the 2.5-mile climb to the top of Round Top Mountain. Along the way, three side trails are passed, all of which connect with the latter half of the ride. Upon the summit, riders are graciously rewarded with a spectacular view of the fertile farmlands of the Penns Valley. The patchwork of fields and forest from this vantage are second only to views from a plane. As you peer down this wide valley, it may be hard to imagine the tunnels and labyrinths that lie only meters below the soil's surface. This valley holds some of the most extensive limestone caves in Pennsylvania and Woodward Cave is only a stones throw from this vantage. You'll also notice the unique 'signal' tower that stands on the summit. The shaky ladder prevents most from climbing to the 360-degree view and I have still not been able to find the purpose of this structure.

Take your time and enjoy the view, you earned it! Returning down from the summit, it's almost all downhill. Finding the descent route is a bit tricky at first, but the landmarks should be obvious. Crossing the huge ditch, the ride resumes on a classic old woods road that slowly meanders down off the mountain. Passing cabins at trail junctions, the ride bears left and crosses Pine Creek across from Negro Hollow. The final spin on Stony Run Road has you grinning all the way back to the trailhead.

Wild Iris

THE RIDE...

0.0 From the intersection of Stony Run and Winklebleck Roads, begin the ride by climbing Winklebleck Road.

0.7 Turn right at the fork, continuing to climb on Round Top Road.

1.2 Pass the Rabbit Shanty Trail on the right

1.8 Pass the Kleckner Spring Trail on the right

2.6 Arrive on the spectacular summit of Round Top Mountain. Check out the incredible views looking due west, over the farms of Penns Valley. Here stands the unique "signal tower" adjacent to the radio towers. What do you think it was used for? Once you're done taking in the views, return down Round Top Road approximately 100 yards, where you will need to turn (bear) left on a grassy old woods road. It may be hard to see the actual trail but it is marked by a large, road-blocking ditch which you will need cross. The trail may be blazed blue.

3.6 Cross the Kleckner Spring Trail at a cabin

4.2 Cross the Rabbit Shanty Trail at a cabin and continue on the other side of the gate.

4.5 Keep left at the fork and soon after (approximately 30 yards) turn left at a T intersection, continuing to follow old woods roads.

5.0 The trail somewhat disappears just above a cabin in the company of some large pines. Continue straight, by carefully riding down along the earthen stairs and crossing a small wooden bridge to Stony Run Road. Turn right on Stony Run Road.

5.5 Arrive back at the trailhead intersection of Stony Run and Winklebleck Roads.

We were taught to believe that the Great Spirit sees and hears everything, and that he never forgets; that hereafter he will give every man a spirit-home according to his deserts... This I believe and my people believe the same.
Chief Joseph, Nez Perce

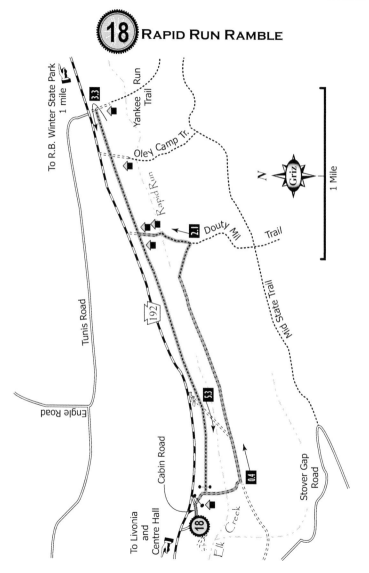

18 RAPID RUN RAMBLE

BIG MOUNTAIN
RIDE 15

Trailhead: **State Game Lands 295 parking area,** 4.2 miles from Lamar. From Exit #173, Lamar on I-80, take State Highway 64 south 1.4 miles to Lamar. In Lamar, turn left on Washington Avenue, which is also marked by a sign for the Lamar National Fish Hatchery. Travel 3.8 miles along Washington Avenue, which will pass the Lamar Fish Hatchery and turn to Narrows Road as it enters State Game Lands 295. Turn left into State Game Lands 295 parking lot, which is marked by tall pines. This lot is just before the guardrail over a small bridge (Cherry Run) and opposite Dale Roach Road. This is the best description I can offer for the trailhead lot, and although it is small, finding it is not as complicated as it seems. **GPS**: N40-59.460' W77-29.600'

Distance: 21.1 mile loop

Time: 3-5 hours

Highlights: Stream crossings, rhododendron tunnels, excellent wildlife viewing, an extended tour of the *Bear Mountain Ride #30*.

Technical Difficulty: 3. The ride predominately follows old woods and forest roads. The descents are a different story, with nice sections of mildly technical singletrack sure to put a smile on any rider's smug mug!

Aerobic Difficulty: Moderate. The initial 7 mile climb is quite enjoyable and mellow, but as the ride follows forestry roads for the last 1.5 miles, it becomes steeper and more strenuous. The 9.6 mile climb is rewarded with 11.5 miles of mostly downhill fun.

Vertical: 2,163 feet of climbing

Climbing Distance: 10.7 miles

Maps: DCNR Bald Eagle State Forest Public Use Map

Land Status: DCNR Bald Eagle State Forest, Pennsylvania Game Commission SGL 295

Ride Notes: Big Mountain is all it's cooked up to be, BIG! The elevation gain is big too, with over 2,000 vertical feet of climbing, this ride is for adventurous weekend warriors looking for good days outing. Not to be missed, and in many ways destined to be a classic ride, Big Mountain offers a true mountain bike experience. The initial half of the ride is uphill, but the grade is mellow enough that it actually becomes an enjoyable climb. Lots of wildlife viewing can be found as you pedal your way through State Game Lands and up into the adjoining State Forest. Making the final push towards Riansares Mountain, the Boiler Trail relieves the gravitational pull, as a sweet 2 mile descent twists and turns on technical trail. A short climb has you retracing some of the route back to the gap in Bear Mountain, where a dirt road turns singletrack after passing through a large field. The final descent is an awesome wide singletrack, involving many stream crossings through deep lush woods.

THE RIDE...

0.0 Begin the ride in the upper left end of the lot on the heavily red-blazed, old woods road. Soon the trail will turn (fork) right on to another old woods road and then turn right again on to a singletrack. The singletrack will cross two foot bridges over Cherry Run.

0.3 After crossing the footbridges, turn left at the T intersection on to the old woods road. Keep right at the fork, and soon after keep right again at another fork, continuing to climb on the wide old woods road.

3.9 Pass an old white car in the woods on the left.

4.5 Come to a small clearing where the old woods road turns to gravel. Follow the gravel road straight, passing a right spuring road that passes through a gap in Bear Mountain.

6.3 Pass around a gate and through a large parking area, continuing straight.

7.4 Turn left on Riansares Road.

8.8 As Riansares Road switchbacks right, pass the Stamm Trail on the left at the switchback elbow.

9.6 After passing a cabin on left, turn right on to the Boiler Trail.

11.7 Turn right on to Low Place Road.

12.0 Turn right at the T intersection on to Rainsares Road.

13.0 Turn left at the fork on to Cherry Run Road, heading back along some familiar trail. In a bit you will pass the parking area and around the gate back into State Game Lands 295.

15.8 In the clearing, turn left at the left spur, following the gravel/dirt road up through the gap in Bear Mountain. Soon after, the trail passes through a large field. Continue along the right edge of the field and pick up the wide singletrack at the far end. Once on the singletrack, keep straight after passing a left spur. As the trail descends on the north bank, it turns hard left and crosses Bear Run (mile 17.5), following along the south bank.

20.6 Pass under the wooden gate and through the small parking area. Turn right on Narrows Road.

21.1 After crossing Cherry Run, turn right into the trailhead lot.

Stellar stream crossings on Bear Run

15 BIG MOUNTAIN

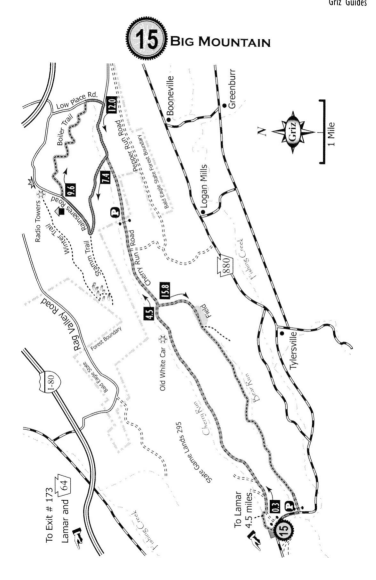

BEAR MOUNTAIN
RIDE 16

Trailhead: **State Game Lands 295 parking area,** 4.2 miles from Lamar. From Exit #173, Lamar on I-80, take State Highway 64 south 1.4 miles to Lamar. In Lamar, turn left on Washington Avenue, which is also marked by a sign for the Lamar National Fish Hatchery. Travel 3.8 miles along Washington Avenue, which will pass the Lamar Fish Hatchery and turn to Narrows Road as it enters State Game Lands 295. Turn left into State Game Lands 295 parking lot, which is marked by tall pines. This lot is just before the guardrail over a small bridge (Cherry Run) and opposite Dale Roach Road. This is the best description I can offer for the trailhead lot, and although it is small, finding it is not as complicated as it seems.
GPS: N40-59.460' W77-29.600'
Distance: 9.7 mile loop.
Time: 1-2 hours.
Highlights: Rhododendron tunnels, stream crossings, excellent wildlife viewing and a true 'deep-woods' feel to the ride.
Technical Difficulty: 2. There are a few spots on the climb and descent that require a little attention but overall the ride is quite smooth. Following old woods roads that are slowly being reclaimed by a healthy forest, the beginning climb tunnels through encroaching rhododendrons. The descent road starts out nice and smooth and slowly degrades to a more loose and bumpy singletrack as it leads to the valley floor.
Aerobic Difficulty: Easy. An awesome ride for folks of all levels and abilities and a true mountain bike ride in every sense of the word. This ride has the 'deep-woods' feel without the extreme elements found on other rides of similar nature. The initial climb is a few miles, but the grade is actually quite enjoyable.
Vertical: 1,142 feet of climbing
Climbing Distance: 5.1 miles
Maps: DCNR Bald Eagle State Forest Public Use Map

Land Status: DCNR Bald Eagle State Forest, Pennsylvania Game Commission SGL 295

Ride Notes: Looping around Bear Mountain this series of mellow old woods roads make up an excellent novice ride. Beginning with a somewhat long but gradual climb, the ride occasionally passes through lush tunnel-like growths of rhododendron. After passing an old car abandoned in the woods the trail soon breaches the notch in Bear Mountain and from there it's all downhill. Passing through a large meadow designed as a game food plot, keep an eye for wildlife both in the field and on the woodland edge. The ride then ducks into the woods on a narrow and more rugged trail, crossing Bear Run to the left and resuming a tight course along the stream. The final leg has you doing the limbo under the old wooden gate and following a short paved section back to the trailhead. A 'must-do' ride for folks of all riding abilities!

Is it ...Bear shit on Big Mountain

or..Big shit on Bear Mountain ?

THE RIDE...

0.0 Begin the ride in the upper left end of the lot on the heavily blazed red, old woods road. Soon the trail will turn (fork) right on to another old woods road and then turn right again on to a singletrack. The singletrack will cross two foot bridges over Cherry Run.

0.3 After crossing the footbridges, turn left at the T intersection on to the old woods road. Keep right at the fork, and soon after keep right again at another fork, continuing to climb on the wide, old woods road.

3.9 Pass an old white car in the woods on the left.

4.5 Come to a small clearing where the old woods road turns to gravel. Turn right at the right-spurring, dirt woods road and follow it southeast through a notch in Bear Mountain.

5.6 Pass through a large field and continue along the right edge and pick up the wide singletrack at the far end. Once on the singletrack, keep straight after passing a left spur.

7.4 The trail turns hard left and crosses Bear Run, following the south bank.

9.2 Pass under the wooden gate and through the parking area, turning right on to the paved Narrows Road.

9.7 After crossing Cherry Run, turn right into the trailhead lot.

...What are you lookin' at? ..and you think you're slow!

16 BEAR MOUNTAIN

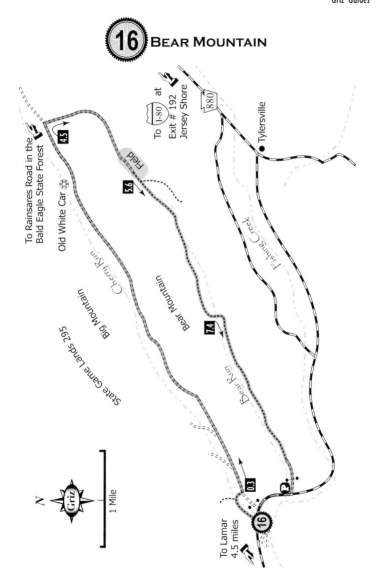

To Rainsares Road in the
Bald Eagle State Forest

Old White Car

4.5

5.6

Field

To I-80 at
Exit # 192
Jersey Shore

880

Tylersville

Fishing Creek

Cherry Run

State Game Lands 295

Big Mountain

Bear Mountain

7.4

Bear Run

0.3

P

16

N

Griz

1 Mile

To Lamar
4.5 miles

HALL MOUNTAIN TRAIL
RIDE 17

Trailhead: **State Highway 447 trailhead**, 24 miles from Lewisburg. From Lewisburg travel west on State Highway 192 for 18 miles. After passing Halfway Lake on the right and R.B. Winter State Park office on the left, continue on State Highway for 5 miles to the village of Livonia and the intersection with State Highway 447. Turn right on State Highway 447 and drive for 1.3 miles to a gravel parking area/pull-out on the right. Note the tall pines behind the lot and a yellow and black metal gate. The ride begins at this pullout.
GPS: N40-59.387' W77-18.310'
Distance: 6.8 mile loop
Time: 1-2 hours
Highlights: Gentle rolling hills, stream crossing, some of the finest wildlife viewing in the area and a 'deep-woods' feel to the ride.
Technical Difficulty: **2+.** The only real challenge is a super-short but steep and somewhat rocky descent down an old tram trail, early in the ride (rated a **4**). This short 3/10 of a mile section is easily hiked through, as the ride resumes on some of the nicest hardpacked woods road in the region.
Aerobic Difficulty: **Easy**. The smooth, hardpacked surface makes for an outstanding ride as your tires roll along this fast surface. The route follows a gentle rise and fall in elevation with only one sharp descent discovered early in the ride.
Vertical: 702 feet of climbing
Climbing Distance: 3.3 miles
Maps: DCNR Bald Eagle State Forest Public Use Map.
Land Status: DCNR Bald Eagle State Forest
Ride Notes: The Hall Mountain Trail has to be the best beginner mountain bike ride in the Bald Eagle. With all the components of a great ride plus a 'deep-woods' feel, this ride is a real showcase for the Central Pennsylvania Mountains. Keep a keen eye for the red blazes that mark much of this ride. Beginning with a grassy

cruise down past an open meadow, the route follows old logging roads through a variety of scenery. The short climb to the summit ridge links with a very old tram trail, which has all but regrown to a narrow singletrack. The short descent may be a bit difficult for some riders due to the rugged nature of the rocky bed, but is easily hiked through to the next section of old logging roads.

Tunneling through a canopy of dense striped maples, the woods here feels deeply intimate and somewhat dark, as the tight growth shades out available light. The old logging road soon opens up and becomes a bit wider as it's hardpacked surface begins to descend, crossing the headwaters of White Deer Creek at a wooden snowmobile bridge. Keep a sharp eye for turkey, grouse and deer along this beautiful stretch of trail. Turning right at the old Birch Still Camp, two separate forestry roads begin to loop you back to the trailhead. The smooth, hardpacked nature of the roads makes the climb seem effortless and before long, the trail resumes on some more old woods roads. Passing around the large road-blocking boulders, the route has you back in the dark woods, occasionally passing small open meadows with colorful songbirds. A quick series of turns deposit you back at the trailhead with a smile from ear to ear. A route sure to please all riders at any level.

THE RIDE...

0.0 From the trailhead lot, ride around the metal gate and continue on the grassy woods road. Note the red blazes.

0.3 At a meadow in a clearing, keep right at a fork(straight), following the red blazes as they lead into the woods. The woods road will narrow as it crests Hall Mountain. At the summit ridge (mile 0.7) the trail turns left and descends an old tram trail which has become a fun, rocky singletrack. At the bottom of the hill, continue to carefully follow the red blazes as they twist thru rocky terrain.

1.0 Turn right at the T intersection and follow the narrow grassy woods road that soon widens.

2.6 Cross a small, wooden snowmobile bridge over White Deer Creek.

3.3 Pass around a gate, cross a small stream and soon after turn right on to Engle Road. Note the Birch Still Camp on the right.

4.1 Turn right at the T on to Tunis Road.

5.5 Turn right on to a grassy woods road, passing around some large boulders and continuing to follow the red blazes.

6.2 Turn left at the T intersection on to another grassy woods road and soon after (approx. 100 yards) turn right on to a somewhat obscure woods road. If you come out to State Highway 447, you missed the turn. The red blazes continue to mark the route.

6.5 Turn left on to a grassy woods road, retracing your route back to the trailhead.

6.8 After passing around the gate, arrive at the trailhead.

Lori enjoying the Hall Mountain Trail

17 HALL MOUNTAIN TRAIL

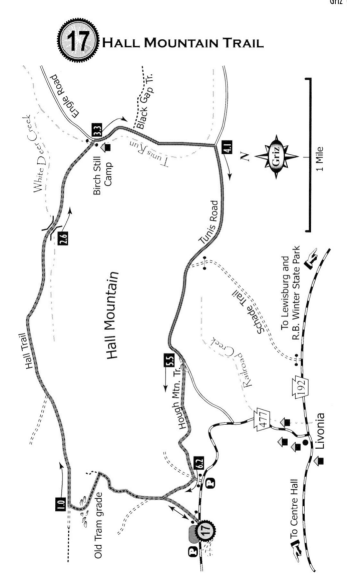

105

Rapid Run Ramble
Ride 18

Trailhead: **Cabin Road trailhead**, 22 miles from Lewisburg. From Lewisburg travel west on State Highway 192 for 18 miles. After passing Halfway Lake on the right and R.B. Winter State Park office on the left, continue on State Highway for 4 miles to Cabin Road, a small marked road on the left. Turn left on Cabin Road and park anywhere along the edge of this horseshoe-shaped road. The ride begins from this location. **GPS**: N40-58.713' W77-16.596'

Distance: 6.0 mile loop including a short out and back section.

Time: 30 minuets to 1 ½ hours

Highlights: Fun and challenging novice loop, variety of trail and terrain types, easy bail-out points on State Highway 192, close to R.B. Winter State Park amenities.

Technical Difficulty: 2. The ride follows a great mix of terrain and trail types with some older reclaimed sections proving to be a bit more challenging (rated **3+**). Bumpy trail and occasional rocks combined with tall grass in sections make for tough going but not impassible for the adventurous novice.

Aerobic Difficulty: Easy. The ride basically follows the 1,660-foot contour as it parallels State Highway 192. The gentle rolling nature and tread surface of the old roads adds a mountain bike element and challenge, not found on Rail-Trail type rides.

Vertical: 441 feet of climbing

Climbing Distance: 3.0 miles

Maps: DCNR Bald Eagle State Forest Public Use Map.

Land Status: DCNR Bald Eagle State Forest

Ride Notes: A step up from easier rides, this route has a bit more flair by tossing out a few fun challenges along the way. The safety net for these obstacles is the paved State Highway 192 that parallels most of the ride. A short hike can have you out on the large shoulder of the highway, which leads back to the trailhead. With that said, the ride covers some diverse trail and surfaces. From hardpacked dirt

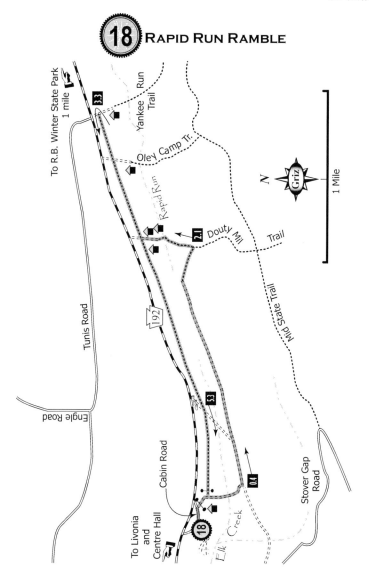

18 RAPID RUN RAMBLE

access road and bumpy old woods roads to grassy singletrack, this route allows you to test your riding ability on a variety of terrains.

The ride departs from the Cabin Road trailhead and begins a fun descent to the low-point of the ride. From there, the route follows a grassy woods road that soon deteriorates to a forgotten logging road enshrouded in saplings. The trail ends on the singletrack of the Douty Mill Trail, past a wet area that is difficult to ride. The lumpy Douty Mill Trail soon turns from tricky singletrack to rough road as it passes a bunch of cabins and joins the red-blazed section of the Central Mountain Trail. Here begins the out-and-back section that terminates on the Yankee Run Trail (Buckhorn Road). Spin around and retrace the route for a bit back to the Douty Mill Trail/Road where the red blazes guide you along the C.M.T. as it parallels the highway.

THE RIDE...

0.0 From the trailhead parking area, head east picking up the dirt road and the red blazes. Soon after you will pass around a gate. Follow the dirt road as it bends right and descends.

0.4 Turn left at the T intersection on to the wide grassy woods road. Pass a left-spur grassy woods road and continue straight as the trail leads into the woods on a narrow old woods road.

2.1 As the trail seems to almost disappear, continue to follow the blazes east. Turn left at a T intersection on to the tiny singletrack of the Douty Mill Trail. Descends this great little trail, crossing a stream through a stand of hemlocks.

2.5 After passing a few cabins, turn right at the 4-way intersection, following the red-blazed trail as it parallels State Highway192 east.

3.3 Arrive at the Yankee Run Trail (Buckhorn Road). This is the turn-around point of the ride, from here follow the red-blazed route as it parallels State Highway 192.

4.1 Cross the Douty Mill Road/Trail.

5.3 Cross a grassy woods road, continuing in the red-blazed trail.

6.0 Merge right on a dirt road, pass around a gate to the trailhead.

HOUGH MOUNTAIN TRAIL
RIDE 19

Trailhead: **Cabin Road trailhead**, 22 miles from Lewisburg. From Lewisburg travel west on State Highway 192 for 18 miles. After passing Halfway Lake on the right and R.B. Winter State Park office on the left, continue on State Highway for 4 miles to Cabin Road, a small marked road on the left. Turn left on Cabin Road and park anywhere along the edge of this horseshoe-shaped road. The ride begins from this location. **GPS**: N40-58.713' W77-16.596'

Distance: 15.1 mile loop

Time: 2-3 hours

Highlights: Varied terrain, awesome weekend-warrior loop, small sections of technical challenges, excellent wildlife viewing, historic old tram trails, close to R.B. Winter State Park amenities.

Technical Difficulty: **2**. A great loop for riders looking for a variety of rideable terrain. Small sections of the Hall Mountain and Schade trails have fun technical challenges like rocks and roots rated at a **4**.

Aerobic Difficulty: **Moderate**. The ride has a bit of climbing and the tread surface is grassy and slow at times. I guess it's fair to say that you'll hafta work a bit to get through this ride but the reward will be well worth it!

Vertical: 1,638 feet of climbing

Climbing Distance: 7.9 miles

Maps: DCNR Bald Eagle State Forest Public Use Map.

Land Status: DCNR Bald Eagle State Forest

Ride Notes: Starting at the Cabin Road trailhead, the ride begins on mellow dirt road and well-maintained grassy woods roads. As the ride continues, the woods roads become a bit more rugged and narrow, leading to the obscure intersection with the Douty Mill Trail. A short but sweet singletrack section puts you parallel with State Highway 192, heading east. Cross the highway and resume on the McCall Field Trail 4-wheel drive road that rambles along joining the Jamboree Trail. A smooth ride ensues as the grassy woods road rolls along the irregular contour of the mountain. Technical challenges present themselves on the Black Gap Trail as it drops down a small drainage on to Engle Road. The Birch Still Camp becomes the landmark for the next turn as the ride follows the Hall Mountain Trail west. Enjoy the silky smooth ride on this awesome stretch and keep a sharp eye for critters along this stretch. An old tram grade presents yet another challenge, leading fearless riders over Hall Mountain on some bumpy terrain. A myriad of old woods roads tries to lose the day-dreaming rider, but hell...this place is so beautiful, it's hard not to drift off! The final bone comes with a wicked-fun descent off the ridge on the Schade Trail, running out across the highway and back to the trailhead.

THE RIDE...

0.0 From the trailhead parking area, head east picking up the dirt road and the red blazes. Soon after you will pass around a gate. Follow the dirt road as it bends right and descends.

0.4 Turn left at the T intersection on to the wide grassy woods road. Pass a left-spur grassy woods road and continue straight as the trail leads into the woods on a narrow old woods road.

2.1 As the trail seems to fade out, turn left at a T intersection, on to the tiny singletrack of the Douty Mill Trail. Descend this great little trail, crossing a stream through a stand of hemlocks.

2.5 After passing a few cabins, turn right at the 4-way intersection, following the red blazed trail as it parallels State Highway192 east.

3.3 Turn left on to Yankee Run Trail (Buckhorn Road) and carefully cross State Highway 192. Resume the ride on Tunis Road, following the red blazes.

3.6 Turn right on to McCall Field Trail (Driveable Trail) doubletrack, and once at the large clearing, follow the trail right as it enters a pine grove on a 4-wheel drive trail.

19 HOUGH MOUNTAIN TRAIL

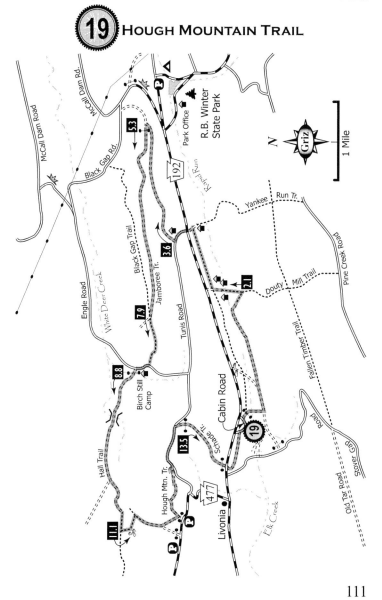

5.3 Turn left on to the Jamboree Trail, a grassy wood road, and pass around a gate.

7.9 Turn left on the somewhat obscure, singletrack Black Gap Trail.

8.6 Turn right on to Engle Road.

8.8 At the Birch Still Camp on the left, turn left on to the dirt road Hall Trail (a.k.a. Kemmerer Trail). Cross over a small stream and pass around a gate, continuing on the grassy woods road.

9.5 Cross a small wooden bridge over White Deer Creek.

10.4 Stay left at a fork, on the wide grassy woods road.

11.1 As the Hall Trail narrows turn left on to the singletrack, continuing to follow the red blazes. The trail will wind through some rocky terrain before climbing a short but steep singletrack. At the crest of the ridge (mile 11.4), resume on a wide grassy woods road which descends off of Hall Mountain.

11.8 Turn left on to a somewhat obscure woods road that is cloaked in thick saplings. If you come to a gate and State Highway 447, you missed the turn!

12.1 Turn left on a grassy woods road and soon after (approx. 100 yards) turn right on to another grassy woods road.

12.8 After passing through the large boulders, turn left on to Tunis Road.

13.5 Turn right on the Schade Trail (grassy woods road) and soon after, pass around a gate.

14.4 After a great descent, follow the trail as it bends left then right, crossing State Highway 192 and resumes on the red-blazed grassy woods road that parallels the highway under a telephone line.

15.0 Arrive on Cabin Road and the trailhead lot.

SHARP BACK TO ROCKY CORNER
RIDE 20

Trailhead: **R.B. Winter State Park Mountain Bike Trailhead,** 18 miles from Lewisburg. From Lewisburg travel west on State Highway 192 for 18 miles. After passing Halfway Lake on the right and R.B. Winter State Park office on the left, the road will come to a unique 4-way intersection. Turn extremely hard right on to Sand Mountain Road and follow it to the State Park parking area. Turn right into the parking area and note the wooden Mountain Bike Trailhead kiosk on the left. The ride begins in the parking lot.

GPS: N40-59.689' W77-11.430'

Distance: 26.3 mile loop

Time: 4-7 hours

Highlights: Incredible vista overlooking the beautiful Penns Valley, historic signal tower, variety of trail types, historic old tram grades, spans 3 separate mountains, R.B Winter State Park and amenities.

Technical Difficulty: **3**. This ride covers a few sections of serious terrain over some serious miles. The tuff sections come along both the east and west ends of the Fallen Timber Trail (rated at **5**). The photos don't do justice to these gnarly rock gardens and the tight shin-shredding singletrack. The steep drop off the Yankee Run Trail will have you gripped as loose rock and burly boulders abound.

Aerobic Difficulty: **Moderate to Strenuous**. A good days outing for rugged riders. The ride covers a moderate amount of vertical and the technical sections slow down even the most honed riders. Enjoy a good workout that spans three mountains over many different trail types with a finish that's sure to please.

Vertical: 3,221 feet of climbing

Climbing Distance: 14.5 miles

Maps: DCNR Bald Eagle State Forest Public Use Map.

Land Status: DCNR Bald Eagle State Forest

Ride Notes: What a long, strange trip indeed! In the immortal words of Jerry, this ride embodies the spirit of the mountains. This ride is long and lean with a mix of forestry roads linking fat sections of woods roads and singletrack. A moderate amount of climbing makes this ride within reach for the average weekend-warrior. Beginning at the State Park trailhead, the ride begins a slow climb to the Fallen Timber Trail that runs atop Shriner Mountain. The wide woods road soon fades to a tight singletrack before dropping off the south side on the Yankee Run Trail. A run out along some forest roads leads to the Dug Trail that skims along the edge of the Hook Natural Area. Keep an eye out for 4-wheel drive vehicles as the route runs west through Negro Hollow and then embarks on another climb. The reward for this easy uphill push is the unique signal tower atop Round Top Mountain and the killer 360 degree views! Old woods roads lead off the mountain and more forestry road follows a grind back up to the Fallen Timber Trail atop Shriner Mountain. What begins as placid singletrack soon turns to a bony ridge ride through numerous small gardens of beautiful white dolomite/limestone rock. The kicker off the ridge is steep and scary drop on the north Yankee Run Trail. An old tram grade is crossed as the Yankee Run continues on a spur of that same grade to the foot of the mountain. Crossing the highway, 4-wheel drive and forestry roads lead to the final descent trail aptly named Rocky Corner. A short spin will have you back to the trailhead smiling with satisfaction and beggin' for a brew.

THE RIDE...

0.0 From the trailhead, turn right on Sand Mountain Road. Soon after (mile 0.2) turn right on to the paved road that leads down past the campground.
0.8 Bear right on to Boyer Gap Road and turn left on State Highway 192.
1.2 Turn right on to Pine Creek Road.
1.7 At left bend in road, turn right on the gated Fallen Timber Trail.

20 SHARPBACK TO ROCKY CORNER

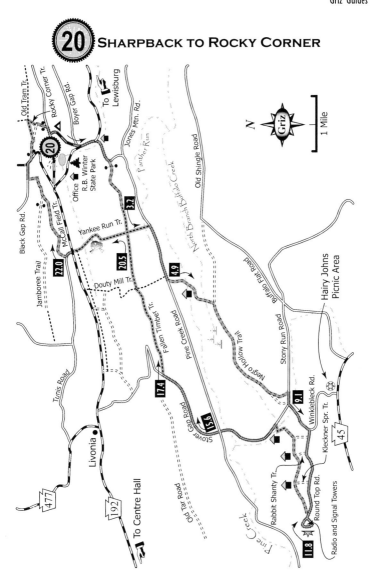

3.2 Turn left on the Yankee Run Trail marked by the chewed-up wooden sign. Soon after you'll cross a faint old woods road (mile 3.5), continuing to descend. **CRUX! May be difficult to find.**

3.7 After crossing over a small wooden foot bridge, turn right on to Pine Creek Road.

4.9 Turn left on to the Dug Trail, which starts out as a dirt 4-wheel drive road. Soon after pass a cabin on the right.

5.9 After crossing the North Branch of Buffalo Creek turn right at the T intersection on to the Negro Hollow Trail (4-wheel drive road).

8.7 Turn right on to Stony Run Road.

9.1 Turn left on to Winklebleck Road.

9.8 Turn right at the fork on to Round Top Road. As you climb this road you'll pass the Rabbit Shanty Trail and the Kleckner Spring Trail, both on your right.

11.8 Arrive on the spectacular summit of Round Top Mountain. Check out the incredible views looking due west, over the farms of Penns Valley. Here stands the unique "signal tower" adjacent to the radio towers. What do you think it was used for? Once you're done taking in the views, return down Round Top Road approximately 100 yards, where you will need to turn (bear) left on a grassy old woods road. It may be hard to see the actual trail but it is marked by a large, road-blocking ditch which you will need cross. The trail may be blazed blue.

12.7 Cross the Kleckner Spring Trail at a cabin

13.3 Cross the Rabbit Shanty Trail at a cabin and continue on the other side of the gate.

13.7 Keep left at the fork and soon after (approximately 30 yards) turn left at a T intersection, continuing to follow old woods roads.

14.1 The trail somewhat **disappears** just above a cabin in the company of some large pines. Continue straight, by carefully riding down along the earthen stairs and crossing a small wooden bridge to Stony Run Road. Turn left on Stony Run Road.

15.6 Cross Pine Creek Road. Stony Gap Road ends here as you continue straight on Stover Gap Road .

17.4 Turn right on the marked Fallen Timber Trail, riding out across this bony ridge.

19.3 Pass the red-blazed Douty Mill Trail on the left.

20.5 Turn left on the Yankee Run Trail and begin the killer descent.

21.0 Cross the Mid State/Brush Hollow Trail.

21.7 Cross State Highway 192 and continue on Tunis Road following the red blazes.

22.0 Turn right on to McCall Field Trail (4-wheel drive road) doubletrack, and once at the large clearing, follow the trail right as it enters a pine grove on a 4-wheel drive trail.

23.6 Merge right on to the grassy doubletrack woods road (Jamboree Trail).

24.2 Turn right on to Black Gap Road. Soon after (mile 24.4) turn right at the T intersection on to McCall Dam Road.

24.5 Turn left on a gated woods road (Boiling Springs Trail).

24.9 After passing under the powerline, turn left on to the Old Tram Trail at the wooden sign.

25.3 Turn right at the 4-way on the blue blazed Rocky Corner Trail and descend.

25.6 Bear left on the Boiling Springs Trail woods road and continue to descend. Soon after, pass around a gate and turn right on to Sand Mountain Road.

26.3 Turn left into the trailhead lot

Salamander Crossing

DOUTY MILL TRAIL
RIDE 21

Trailhead: **R.B. Winter State Park Mountain Bike Trailhead,** 18 miles from Lewisburg. From Lewisburg travel west on State Highway 192 for 18 miles. After passing Halfway Lake on the right and R.B. Winter State Park office on the left, the road will come to a unique 4-way intersection. Turn extremely hard right on to Sand Mountain Road and follow it to the State Park parking area. Turn right into the parking area and note the wooden Mountain Bike Trailhead kiosk on the left. The ride begins in the parking lot.
GPS: N40-59.689' W77-11.430'
Distance: 11.0 mile loop
Time: 2-3 hours
Highlights: Tricky, tough and technical trail, steep descent, short but stout loop, R.B. Winter State Park amenities.
Technical Difficulty: 3. Parts of the ride follow easy terrain but there are many technical surprises. The Fallen Timber Trail is a good warm-up for the super-steep descent of the Douty Mill Trail, rated at a **5**. The ride mellows a bit before the finale of the Rocky Corner Trail descent, also rated at a **5**.
Aerobic Difficulty: Moderate. The ride covers a bit of climbing in a short amount of distance. The terrain is challenging as well, with rocky, rooted and steep sections sure to please any hammerhead.
Vertical: 1,345 feet of climbing
Climbing Distance: 6.2 miles
Maps: DCNR Bald Eagle State Forest Public Use Map.
Land Status: DCNR Bald Eagle State Forest
Ride Notes: The Douty Mill Trail is one of the many highlighted short trails on the ride, each one of these having their own unique flavor. The ride begins at R.B. Winter and passes the campground on it's way out of the park. Crossing State Highway 192, the ride climbs a forest road to the gated Fallen Timber Trail. As the Fallen Timber Trail slowly climbs Shriner Mountain, it soon becomes

more constricted and passes the Yankee Run Trail. The excitement begins for downhill junkies as the Douty Mill Trail screams off the ridge on tight and rocky terrain. It's over all too soon as the ride crosses State Highway 192 and resumes a rolling ramble along the McCall Field Trail. The final cheap thrill is found on the Old Tram to Rocky Corner Trails as this short but sweet technical treat passes the Boiling Spring and rolls back to the trailhead.

THE RIDE...

0.0 From the trailhead, turn right on Sand Mountain Road. Soon after (mile 0.2) turn right on to the paved road that leads down past the campground.

0.8 Bear right on to Boyer Gap Road and turn left on State Highway 192.

1.2 Turn right on to Pine Creek Road.

1.7 At the left bend in the road, turn right on to the gated Fallen Timber Trail.

3.2 Cross over the Yankee Run Trail marked by the chewed-up wooden sign.

4.4 Turn right on to the **somewhat obscure** Douty Mill Trail. The trail may be marked with a sign but will be blazed with the red-blazes and the triangular multi-use signs.

4.6 Cross over the Mid State/Brush Hollow Trail, continue to descend.

5.5 As the trail dumps out on to a woods road, pass some cabins and just before coming out on to State Highway 192, turn right on to the red-blazed trail.

6.0 Cross a woods road.

6.3 Turn left on to Yankee Run Trail (dirt road) and carefully cross State Highway 192. Resume the ride on Tunis Road, following the red blazes.

6.6 Turn right on to McCall Field Trail doubletrack, and once at the large clearing, follow the trail right as it enters a pine grove on a 4-

wheel drive trail.

8.3 Merge right on to the grassy doubletrack woods road of the Jamboree Trail.

8.9 Turn right on to Black Gap Road. Soon after (mile 9.1) turn right on to McCall Dam Road.

9.2 Turn left on a gated woods road, the Boiling Springs Trail.

9.6 After passing under the powerline, turn left on to the Old Tram Trail at the wooden sign.

10.0 Turn right at the 4-way on the blue blazed Rocky Corner Trail and descend.

10.3 Bear left on the Boiling Springs Trail woods road and continue to descend. Soon after pass around a gate and turn right on to Sand Mountain Road.

11.0 Turn left into the trailhead lot.

Gazing down the bars at some killer singletrac

20 SHARPBACK TO ROCKY CORNER

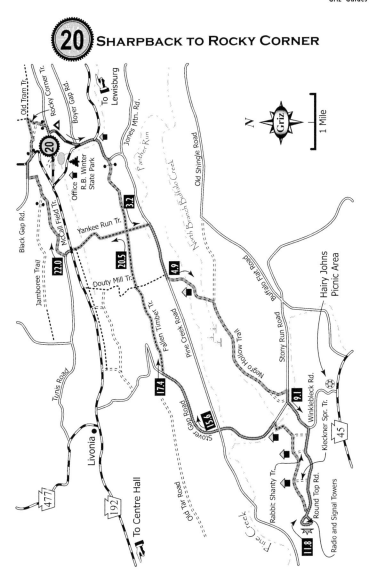

FALLEN TIMBER TO YANKEE RUN
RIDE 22

Trailhead: **R.B. Winter State Park Mountain Bike Trailhead,** 18 miles from Lewisburg. From Lewisburg travel west on State Highway 192 for 18 miles. After passing Halfway Lake on the right and R.B. Winter State Park office on the left, the road will come to a unique 4-way intersection. Turn extremely hard right on to Sand Mountain Road and follow it to the State Park parking area. Turn right into the parking area and note the wooden Mountain Bike Trailhead kiosk on the left. The ride begins in the parking lot.

GPS: N40-59.689' W77-11.430'

Distance: 23.7 mile loop

Time: 4-6 hours

Highlights: Technical rocky singletrack, steep scary descents, variety of trail types, R.B. Winter State Park and amenities.

Technical Difficulty: 3. The Fallen Timber and Yankee Run Trails pose the biggest threat to shreddin' your shins and breaking your bones. The rest of the ride is a bit mellower with small sections of the Shade and Hall Trails throwing down some lunker stones. Much of the ride is linked with old woods and forestry roads.

Aerobic Difficulty: Strenuous. Lots of climbing, long miles and rough terrain make this a rugged ride for burly bikers. If 'tuff-stuff' is what you long for, this ride has got it going on!

Vertical: 2,712 feet of climbing

Climbing Distance: 12.7 miles

Maps: DCNR Bald Eagle State Forest Public Use Map.

Land Status: DCNR Bald Eagle State Forest

Ride Notes: Saddle-up and strap in because this ride is gonna get rough. Starting out from R.B.Winter, the initial climb takes you past the Boiling Spring and up on to Sand Mountain. Forestry roads lead to the unmarked Jamboree Trail that continues beyond a gate and rolls above the Black Gap drainage. The first fun technical section comes with a short screaming descent down the Black Gap Trail.

More forestry roads and grassy woods roads embark on another climb to an old tram grade. Testing your technical skills, rocky singletrack climbs the short but steep north face of Hall Mountain and descends down the more gentle south side via a narrow grassy woods road. A few twisty sections along the Hough Mountain Trail connect with forestry road to another kicker descent down the Schade Trail. Crossing State Highway 192, the ride resumes on more grassy roads as it begins the final long climb to the summit ridge of Shriner Mountain and the Fallen Timber Trail. Atop the ridge is the place to rest-up and gear-up for the technical finale of the ride. Three miles of "rough n' tumble" bony ridge riding along the Fallen Timber Trail and a mile-long sketchy descent back down to the highway will have you pulling tricks for treats. Crossing the highway again, the ride hooks into the 4-wheel drive road of the McCall Field Trail and soon links with the Jamboree Trail. The remainder of the route retraces some familiar terrain with a chilling drop down the Rocky Corner Trail and a spin back to the trailhead.

THE RIDE...

0.0 From the trailhead, turn right on Sand Mountain Road and follow it straight as the road surface changes to hardpacked dirt.

0.5 Turn left on to a dirt road that passes Boiling Spring Camp on the right and soon after passes around a gate.

0.7 Pass under the powerline as the trail bend left. Soon the trail will pass a small right spur that leads to the Boiling Spring enclosure. Check it out if you have time!

1.0 After climbing the steep hill and passing around a gate, follow the woods road under a powerline as it begins to descend.

1.4 Pass around a gate and turn right on McCall Dam Road. Soon after (mile 1.5) turn left on Black Gap Road.

1.7 Turn left on to the doubletrack woods road marked as a "Driveable Trail"

2.3 Keep right at the fork, and pass around a metal gate (Jamboree Trail).

4.8 Turn left on the somewhat obscure singletrack of the Black Gap Trail.

5.6 Turn right on to Engle Road.

5.8 At the Birch Still Camp on the left, turn left on to the dirt road Hall Trail (a.k.a. Kemmerer Trail). Cross over a small stream and pass around a gate, continuing on the grassy woods road.

6.5 Cross a small wooden bridge over White Deer Creek.

7.4 Stay left at a fork, on the wide grassy woods road.

8.1 As the Hall Trail narrows, turn left on to the singletrack, continuing to follow the red blazes. The trail will wind through some rocky terrain before climbing a short but steep singletrack, which was at one time an old tram trail. At the crest of the ridge (mile 8.4), resume on a wide grassy woods road which descends off of Hall Mountain.

8.8 Turn left on to a somewhat obscure woods road that is cloaked in thick saplings. If you come to a gate and State Highway 447, you missed the turn!

9.1 Turn left on a grassy woods road and soon after (approx. 100 yards) turn right on to another grassy woods road.

9.8 After passing through the large boulders, turn left on to Tunis Road.

10.5 Turn right on to Schade Trail (grassy woods road) and soon after, pass around a gate.

11.4 After a great descent, follow the trail as it bends left then right, crossing State Highway 192 and resumes on the red-blazed grassy woods road that parallels the highway under a telephone line.

11.9 Ride out along Cabin Road and reenter the woods on the red-blazed dirt road. Follow the road as it descends, crosses a small creek and reascends the hill.

12.4 Turn right at the T intersection on the grassy woods road.

13.0 Pass around a gate and turn left on Stover Gap Road.

14.8 Turn left on the marked Fallen Timber Trail, riding out across this bony ridge.

22 FALLEN TIMBER TO YANKEE RUN

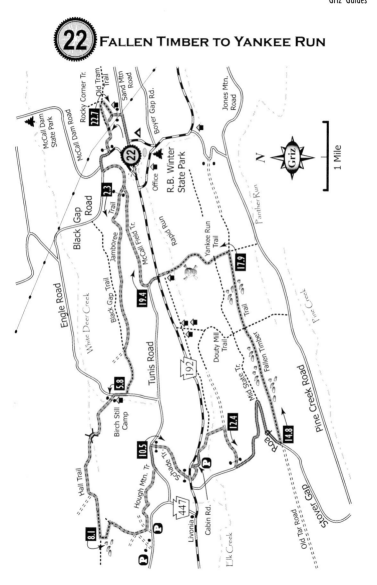

16.6 Pass the somewhat obscure red-blazed Douty Mill Trail.

17.9 Turn left on the **somewhat obscure** Yankee Run Trail and begin the killer descent.

18.4 Cross the Mid State/Brush Hollow Trail.

19.1 Cross State Highway 192 and continue on Tunis Road following the red blazes.

19.4 Turn right on to McCall Field Trail (Driveable Trail) doubletrack, and once at the large clearing, follow the trail right as it enters a pine grove on a 4-wheel drive trail.

21.0 Merge right on to the grassy doubletrack woods road (Jamboree Trail).

21.6 Turn right on to Black Gap Road. Soon after (mile 21.8) turn right on to McCall Dam Road.

22.0 Turn left on a gated woods road, the Boiling Springs Trail.

22.3 After passing under the powerline, turn left on to the Old Tram Trail at the wooden sign.

22.7 Turn right at the 4-way on the blue blazed Rocky Corner Trail and descend.

23.0 Bear left on the Boiling Springs Trail woods road and continue to descend. Soon after pass around a gate and turn right on to Sand Mountain Road.

23.7 Turn left into the trailhead lot

"Gnarl Karl"

Fallen Timber Trail

BOILING SPRINGS
RIDE 23

Trailhead: **R.B. Winter State Park Mountain Bike Trailhead**, 18 miles from Lewisburg. From Lewisburg travel west on State Highway 192 for 18 miles. After passing Halfway Lake on the right and R.B. Winter State Park office on the left, the road will come to a unique 4-way intersection. Turn extremely hard right on to Sand Mountain Road and follow it to the State Park parking area. Turn right into the parking area and note the wooden Mountain Bike Trailhead kiosk on the left. The ride begins in the parking lot.

GPS: N40-59.689' W77-11.430'

Distance: 11.9 mile loop

Time: 1-3 hours

Highlights: The geologic wonder of the Boiling Springs, R.B. Winter State Park amenities, excellent ride for almost all levels of riders.

Technical Difficulty: 1. Much of the ride follows smooth treads on grassy woods roads and hardpacked forestry roads. There is one short downhill section on the Black Gap Trail that is quite challenging at a rating of **3+**.

Aerobic Difficulty: Easy to Moderate. The initial step climb up past Boiling Springs may cause some riders to dismount and hike up this challenging grade. Once atop Sand Mountain, the ride rolls along on gentle grades with many fun ups and downs. Don't forget that the ride descends the initial steep climb so enjoy the 'free-ride' home.

Vertical: 1,317 feet of climbing

Climbing Distance: 5.9 miles

Maps: DCNR Bald Eagle State Forest Public Use Map.

Land Status: DCNR Bald Eagle State Forest

Ride Notes: What a great ride located in an incredible setting! Revised and improved from my second guide, *Mountain Biking Pennsylvania*, This version includes an extra link of trail along with an improved digital map and mileage log produced with GPS software. The ride follows a fun but challenging route out of the State Park and up on Sand Mountain while passing the geologic wonder of the Boiling Springs. Once on top of the mountain a few short links connect the McCall Field Trail with the Jamboree Trail as the grassy woods roads roll along. A short but challenging section of the Black Gap Trail follows a rocky course before the ride continues on smooth forest roads. Back on the McCall Field Trail the ride follows this rough 4-wheel drive road as it reconnects to some familiar trail atop Sand Mountain. The final reward is the fun downhill past the Boiling Springs and back to the trailhead. The Boiling Springs are located in a 'chicken-coop' type enclosure to prevent the contamination of the spring. Upon close inspection, you can just about see the 'boiling' effect of the artesian pressure. Sometimes due to the light conditions it's hard to see, so head down to the beach along the Halfway Lake's northwest shore. Just off the footpath, there is another boiling spring appropriately called the 'Little Bubbler'. Here you can catch a glimpse of this unique feature and get to see just why the lake is so damn cold!

THE RIDE...

0.0 From the trailhead lot, head out to and turn right on Sand Mountain Road.

0.6 Turn left on a dirt road, passing the Boiling Spring Camp and around a gate on the Boiling Spring Trail. Soon the trail passes the enclosed Boiling Springs on the right.

1.0 After climbing the steep hill, pass around a gate. Soon pass the Old Tram Trail on the right and ride under the powerline.

1.4 Pass around a gate and turn right on McCall Dam Road. Soon after (mile 1.6) turn left on Black Gap Road.

1.7 Turn left on the McCall Field Trail "Driveable Road".

23 BOILING SPRINGS

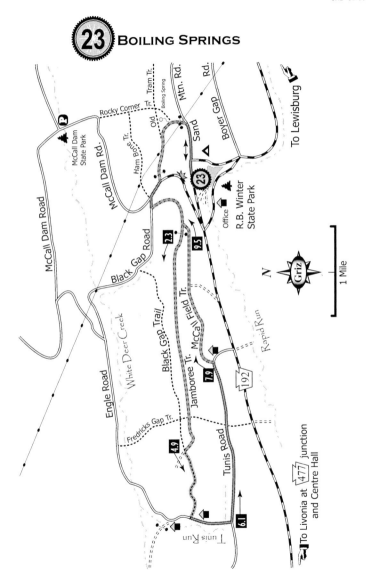

2.3 Right at the fork and pass around a gate on the Jamboree Trail.

4.9 Turn left on to a somewhat obscure red-blazed singletrack of the Black Gap Trail.

5.6 After a great descent, turn left on Engle Road.

6.1 Turn left on to Tunis Road.

7.9 Turn left on the McCall Field Trail "Driveable Road" and follow the trail and red-blazes right at a clearing as they head into a pine forest.

8.8 Pass a right spur woods road at a small clearing.

9.5 Merge right on to the grassy woods road, continuing on the McCall Field Trail.

10.1 Turn right on Black Gap Road. Soon after at mile 10.3, turn right on to the McCall Dam Road.

10.5 Turn left on the Boiling Springs Trail and pass around a gate. Retrace the route back to the trailhead.

11.3 Turn right on Sand Mountain Road

11.9 Turn left into the trailhead lot.

Boiling Springs enclosure

COWBELL HOLLOW
RIDE 24

Trailhead: **R.B. Winter State Park Mountain Bike Trailhead**, 18 miles from Lewisburg. From Lewisburg travel west on State Highway 192 for 18 miles. After passing Halfway Lake on the right and R.B. Winter State Park office on the left, the road will come to a unique 4-way intersection. Turn extremely hard right on to Sand Mountain Road and follow it to the State Park parking area. Turn right into the parking area and note the wooden Mountain Bike Trailhead kiosk on the left. The ride begins in the parking lot.

GPS: N40-59.689' W77-11.430'

Distance: 29.9 mile loop

Time: 4-6 hours

Highlights: The <u>must-do</u> '**Classic**' mountain bike ride, tons of technical challenges, spectacular vistas, old tram grades, ridge and valley riding, R.B. Winter State Park amenities.

Technical Difficulty: 4. The ride runs the gamut of tough trail. Big logs, loose rocks, slick roots, and sketchy steep terrain are just some of the fun highlights to be found. The most burly section is the 4.5 miles stretch of the Top Mountain Trail, which is sure to beat on harebrained hammerheads.

Aerobic Difficulty: Strenuous. Significant gains in elevation and extremely demanding terrain are what can be expected. The ride demands endurance, fitness, strength and skill. Do you have what it takes?

Vertical: 3,674 feet of climbing

Climbing Distance: 15.3 miles

Maps: DCNR Bald Eagle State Forest Public Use Map.

Land Status: DCNR Bald Eagle State Forest

Ride Notes: Even before this ride was published in *Mountain Biking Pennsylvania*, it was truly a classic ride. A few years later and with the help of GPS and digital mapping the 'Cowbell' gets a fresh new look with a few minor changes. The new route includes a classic old tram grade on the Black Gap Trail, a new departure trail from the trailhead and the omission of the Bake Oven Trail. Hardcore rides breed hardcore riders and the Cowbell Hollow does just that. Leaving the trailhead the ride quickly gains Sand Mountain and rolls out to the Black Gap Trail. A killer descent on this rocky old tram grade leads to the next singletrack along White Deer Creek. Slick roots sprawl across the trail like the arms of an angry octopus and moss-covered rocks dot the trail like soft green turtles. After a short forest road spin, the singletrack continues on the Stony Hollow Trail and resumes back on the forest road, heading for Cowbell Hollow. This tight, twisty and rolling singletrack is the finest around and as it descends the hollow, the ride gets downright rough in a rocky drainage. A stiff climb up Nittany Mountain will soon seem easy as the ride continues out along the tuff Top Mountain Trail. A short downhill and a bit more climbing has you at the Sand Mountain Fire Tower where the final descent coasts back to the trailhead.

 ## THE RIDE...

0.0 From the trailhead lot, head out to and turn right on Sand Mountain Road.

0.6 Turn left on a dirt road, passing the Boiling Spring Camp and around a gate on the Boiling Spring Trail. Soon the trail passes the enclosed Boiling Springs on the right.

1.0 After climbing the steep hill, pass around a gate. Soon pass the Old Tram Trail on the right and ride under the powerline.

1.4 Pass around a gate and turn right on McCall Dam Road. Soon after (mile 1.6) turn left on Black Gap Road.

1.7 Turn left on the McCall Field Trail "Driveable Road".

2.3 Keep right at the fork and pass around a gate on the Jamboree Trail.

4.9 Turn hard right on to a somewhat obscure red-blazed singletrack of the Black Gap Trail.

24 COWBELL HOLLOW

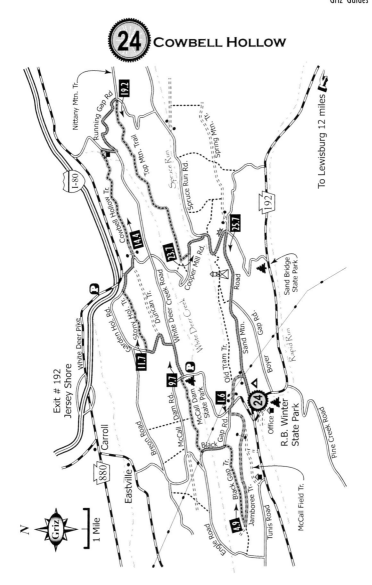

6.2 Pass a pipeline opening.

7.2 Cross a small wooden foot bridge and turn left on Black Gap Road.

7.9 After crossing a bridge over White Deer Creek, turn right on the White Deer Creek Trail at the bend in the road.

9.7 Turn right on to McCall Dam Road and immediately turn left on White Deer Creek Road. The McCall Dam State Park is located near this intersection and is a great place to regroup and take a rest.

10.5 Turn left climbing Garden Hollow Road.

11.7 Turn right on the Stony Hollow Trail. The Stony Hollow Trail may be blazed, but if not it is marked by a pair of large boulders at a narrow grassy inset.

13.4 Turn right on to Garden Hollow Road.

13.8 Turn right at the fork, climbing Coopers Mill Road.

14.4 Turn left on the gated Cowbell Hollow Trail and follow the woods road as it narrows and becomes a singletrack after a clearing. This section is the "Tits", so send it hard!

17.1 The trail dumps out at a cabin. Politely ride around the edge of the property to a dirt driveway and out across a bridge to the road. Turn right on White Deer Creek Road.

17.5 Turn hard left climbing on Running Gap Road.

19.2 At the crest of the Nittany Mountain, turn right on the Top Mountain Trail, opposite the forest road intersection. You might wanna' relieve your bladder first!

23.7 Keep left at a fork marked by a grassy campsite complete with fire ring and ride over a dirt berm. The trail becomes a wide singletrack as it descends.

23.9 Turn left on Coopers Mill Road, continuing to descend a bit.

25.7 After passing the Cooper Mill Vista on the left, turn right at the 4-way intersection on Sand Mountain Road.

26.7 Pass the Sand Mountain Fire Tower on the right and begin a well-earned descent.

29.9 Turn left into the trailhead.

Old Tram Trail
Ride 25

Trailhead: **R.B. Winter State Park Mountain Bike Trailhead**, 18 miles from Lewisburg. From Lewisburg travel west on State Highway 192 for 18 miles. After passing Halfway Lake on the right and R.B. Winter State Park office on the left, the road will come to a unique 4-way intersection. Turn extremely hard right on to Sand Mountain Road and follow it to the State Park parking area. Turn right into the parking area and note the wooden Mountain Bike Trailhead kiosk on the left. The ride begins in the parking lot.

GPS: N40-59.689' W77-11.430'

Distance: 6.5 mile loop

Time: 30 minuets to 1 ½ hours

Highlights: One of the best preserved historic logging tram grades in the area, great 'deep-woods' feel, technically sustained sections, a 'Zen'-like rock riding experience, R.B. Winter State Park amenities.

Technical Difficulty: 4+. Relentless sections of sustained rocky tram bed comprise the bulk of the ride. The Old Tram trail follows the rocky and rooted bed of an old logging tram railway. The original ballast bed is littered with rock of all sizes, many of which rock and roll as you ride through them. The rest of the ride is forestry road, which return you to the trailhead at Mach speed.

Aerobic Difficulty: Moderate to Strenuous. Pumping and pedaling your way through an old tram grade is not easy. Your head and heart have to be into the ride, as it demands extreme attention along the technical stretches. Your butt and bladder will take a beating too, even on a "softiee special".

Vertical: 559' elevation gain

Climbing Distance: 2.6 miles

Maps: DCNR Bald Eagle State Forest Public Use Map.

Land Status: DCNR Bald Eagle State Forest

Ride Notes: A short classic ride on a classic piece of Bald Eagle forest history. Built back in the late 1800's to haul logs from the Sand Mountain drainage, these tram grades served a short but stout life during this industrious era. When the hills were stripped bare (hence the name of the mountain to the north of Sand Mountain, Naked Mountain), these tram grades were abandoned to the woods. Over one hundred years later, trails like the Old Tram Trail have provided outdoor recreation pathways for folks like us with the need to get back into the heart of the woods. Third generation woods and overgrown trail have replaced what was once a barren and decimated landscape. Only the rock that lines the bed exists in its original state. Brutal but rideable, many of these well-preserved tram grades require a certain finesse and skill to successfully ride

atop them. A combination of speed, torque, a light front-end and a general 'lightness-of-being' are necessary to pedal through the madness. Once you get it down, it's truly an enlightening experience. This short ride sets out from the park and climbs a short, steep hill to gain the Old Tram Trail.

From here, the ride follows a descending grade between Naked and Sand Mountains on the rocky ballast. A sharp switchback and more rock tests your skills on an uphill section before cresting Sand Mountain and exiting on Sand Mountain Road. The final leg is a well-earned smooth cruise on forest road to the trailhead.

THE RIDE...

0.0 From the trailhead, turn right on Sand Mountain Road, following it straight as the road surface changes to hardpacked dirt.

0.5 Turn left on to a dirt road that passes Boiling Spring Camp on the

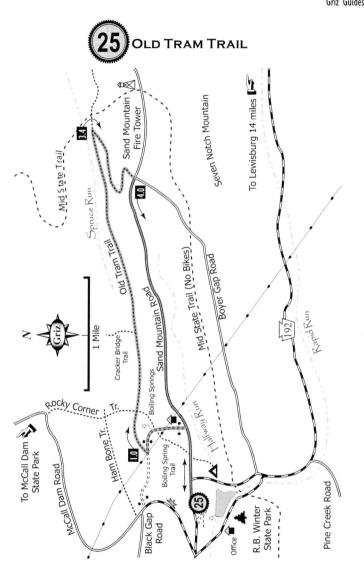

25 OLD TRAM TRAIL

right and soon after passes around a gate.

0.7 Pass under the powerline as the trail bends left. Soon the trail will pass a small right spur that leads to the Boiling Spring enclosure. Check it out if you have time!

1.0 After climbing the steep hill and passing around a gate, bear right to find the Old Tram Trail marked by the wooden forestry signs. Turn right on the Old Tram Trail.

1.4 Pass the Rocky Corner Trail.

2.0 Cross the Cracker Bridge Trail

3.4 Turn hard right at a switchback, following the red-blazed tram grade as it climbs.

4.0 Turn right on to Sand Mountain Road at the intersection with Boyer Gap Road and descend to the trailhead.

6.5 Trailhead.

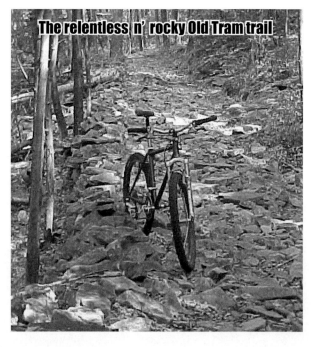
The relentless n' rocky Old Tram trail

BUFFALO MOUNTAIN
RIDE 26

Trailhead: **R.B. Winter State Park Mountain Bike Trailhead**, 18 miles from Lewisburg. From Lewisburg travel west on State Highway 192 for 18 miles. After passing Halfway Lake on the right and R.B. Winter State Park office on the left, the road will come to a unique 4-way intersection. Turn extremely hard right on to Sand Mountain Road and follow it to the State Park parking area. Turn right into the parking area and note the wooden Mountain Bike Trailhead kiosk on the left. The ride begins in the parking lot.

GPS: N40-59.689' W77-11.430'

Distance: 21.8 mile loop

Time: 2-4 hours

Highlights: Steep sections of sketchy singletrack, long miles of forest roads, steepest vertical, old tram trails, Buffalo Mountain summit, R.B. Winter State Park amenities and a pair of loops with options to shorten the ride.

Technical Difficulty: **3+.** The steep sections of singletrack on the Grosses Gap and Bear Gap Trails are blessed with small, loose rock and off-camber logs. The Cracker Bridge and Old Tram Trails follows the rocky and rooted bed of an old tram railway, rated at **4+.** The original ballast bed is paved with rock of all sizes, many of which rock and roll as you ride through them. The rest of the ride cruises forestry road, which makes the loop roll along a bit faster.

Aerobic Difficulty: **Moderate**: The ride is set up so that you ride the mellow forest roads on the climbs and hammer the steep, scary stuff on the descent. There is definitely a bunch of climbing but its spread out over many miles, keeping the grind to a tolerable grade.

Vertical: 3,177 feet of climbing

Climbing Distance: 13.8 miles

Maps: DCNR Bald Eagle State Forest Public Use Map.

Land Status: DCNR Bald Eagle State Forest

Ride Notes: This ride, like many other rides in this guide, covers a lot of historical terrain. Buffalo Mountain is aptly named after the extinct woodland buffalo that once migrated down through the gap near the village of Buffalo Crossings. It's hard to imagine the thunderous hooves of hundreds of migrating buffalo stampeding down through this quaint valley. Although no real tangible evidence of the Woodland Buffalo has been found around here, it is believed that this region was their last stronghold in Pennsylvania. Beginning with sections of the Cracker Bridge and Old Tram Trails, these old logging rail grades were created back in the late 1800's to transport timber from ridge tops to valley floors. Climbing the Sand Mountain Ridge, old woods roads lead out along the western flank of Buffalo Mountain. A short but extremely exciting loop descends the dark bowels of Bear Gap and climbs back out on the rugged Sand Mountain Road. Running the Buffalo Ridge a second time to the true summit of Buffalo Mountain, Grosses Gap Trail becomes your one-way ticket to bottom with one of the steepest vertical drops, over 1,100 feet in less than one mile! Following an old woods road to Spruce Run Road, the ride then climbs out on smooth, fast forest roads to the trailhead. This ride is a great challenge for intermediate riders looking for a good days outing. The vertical elevations are mild and the trails are in great shape.

THE RIDE...

0.0 Head out from the trailhead lot and turn right on to Sand Mountain Road, which soon turns to dirt.
2.4 Turn left on to the Cracker Bridge Trail, which is located at a 4x4" post near the intersection of Sand Mountain and Boyer Gap Roads. The post is marked "Cracker Bridge Trail" on the east face of the post. The trail climbs up into the woods heading left then turns right, crossing Sand Mountain Ridge. You will also note the red blazes and a cross-country skier and the multi-use trail signs.

26 BUFFALO MOUNTAIN

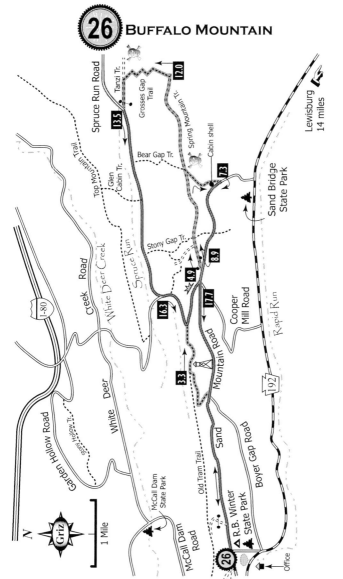

Spruce Run Road

Tanzi Tr.

Grosses Gap Trail

12.0

13.5

Lewisburg
14 miles

Spring Mountain Tr.

Cabin shell

Top Mountain Trail

Bear Gap Tr.

Glen Cabin Tr.

7.3

Sand Bridge State Park

Creek Road

White Deer Creek

Spruce Run

Stony Gap Tr.

8.9

4.9

I-80

16.3

17.7

Cooper Mill Road

Rapid Run

192

3.3

Mountain Road

Garden Hollow Road

White Deer

Stony Hollow Tr.

Old Tram Trail

Sand

Boyer Gap Road

McCall Dam State Park

N Griz

1 Mile

McCall Dam Road

R.B. Winter State Park

26

Office

141

3.3 At a left-hand switchback, keep straight, following the narrow Old Tram Trail into the woods. You will soon see blue blazes on the trees letting you know you're on the Old Tram Trail. <u>DO NOT</u> follow the red blazes and icon signs as they switchback left!

4.1 Turn right on to Cooper Mill Road and climb, soon passing the Cooper Mill vista on the left.

4.8 Turn left at the 4-way intersection on to Buffalo Mountain Road Trail. Soon after turn left on to a gated woods road. This is the Spring Mountain Trail.

5.2 Keep right at a fork, staying on the Spring Mountain Trail. Soon after you will cross the Stony Gap Trail on the left, a blue blazed skinny old woods road.

6.5 At a large clearing (old log skidder landing), turn hard right (120 degrees) at the faint 4-way intersection onto the somewhat obscure singletrack which is blazed blue. This is the Bear Gap Trail and it soon becomes more obvious. Another clue in finding this trail is that on the opposite side, the Bear Gap Trail is a very obvious grassy woods road.

7.3 After an awesome descent, cross a rocky stream and pass and old cabin shell on the right. Soon after, pass some stone ruins on left and turn right on to Sand Mountain Road.

8.9 Turn right at the second right-spurring old woods road, passing around the gate again. Soon after keep right at the fork, riding out on the Spring Mountain Trail again.

10.5 Pass a spurring trail that merges in from the right and soon after pass the Bear Gap Trail 4-way intersection.

12.0 The old woods road ends at a small circle. Turn left on to the tight singletrack of the Grosses Gap Trail, get ready to drop some serious vert!

13.0 Turn left at the T intersection on to the grassy old woods road, the Tanzi Trail.

13.5 After passing around a gate, turn left on to Spruce Gap Road. As you ride on, the route will pass the Bear Gap Trail on the left, the Glen Cabin Trail on the right and the Stony Gap Trail on the left.

16.3 Turn left at the T intersection on to Cooper Mill Road.

17.7 Turn right at the 4-way intersection on to Sand Mountain Road.

18.6 Pass the fire tower on the right, at the summit of Sand Mountain. As the road descends, the route passes Boyer Gap Road on the left.

21.8 Turn left into the trailhead lot.

ROUND KNOB TO STONY GAP
RIDE 27

Trailhead: **R.B. Winter State Park Mountain Bike Trailhead**, 18 miles from Lewisburg. From Lewisburg travel west on State Highway 192 for 18 miles. After passing Halfway Lake on the right and R.B. Winter State Park office on the left, the road will come to a unique 4-way intersection. Turn extremely hard right on to Sand Mountain Road and follow it to the State Park parking area. Turn right into the parking area and note the wooden Mountain Bike Trailhead kiosk on the left. The ride begins in the parking lot.

GPS: N40-59.689' W77-11.430'

Distance: 11.9 mile loop

Time: 2-3 hours

Highlights: One of the best preserved historic logging tram grades in the area, great 'deep-woods' feel, technically sustained sections, a 'Zen'-like rock riding experience, an old tram-truck wheel from the early logging days.

Technical Difficulty: 3. Relentless sections of sustained rocky tram bed comprise the roughly half of the ride. The Old Tram Trail follows the rocky and rooted bed of an old logging tram railway. The original ballast bed is littered in sections with rock of all sizes, many of which rock and roll as you ride through them at Grade **4**. The climb up around Round Knob isn't too shabby with it's own mix of rock and root. The descent down into Stony Gap is quite a

143

rip with a handful of short but brutal rock gardens at Grade **5+.**

Aerobic Difficulty: Moderate to Strenuous. Pumping and pedaling your way through one old tram grade is not easy, let alone three! Your head and heart have to be into the ride, as it demands extreme attention along the technical stretches. Your butt and bladder will take a beating too. The ride has some fun but demanding climbs that complete this adventurous outing 'round Round Knob.

Vertical: 1,405 feet of climbing

Climbing Distance: 5.4 miles

Maps: DCNR Bald Eagle State Forest Public Use Map.

Land Status: DCNR Bald Eagle State Forest

Ride Notes: Round Knob is fun extension on the *Old Tram Trail (Ride # 25)* with some great additional singletrack sections on challenging terrain. The ride not only covers the entire length of the old tram grade on the north face of Sand Mountain but hits two other 'hidden highways' on the south shoulder of Round Knob. One of the coolest finds on this route is an old steel tram-truck wheel. This old cast wheel is embedded in the moss-covered yard of the Stony

Gap cabin. Very little steel and iron has remained in the woods from the logging times and this icon stands as a visual reminder of the logging era. The ride begins by climbing up on Sand Mountain and jumping right on the Old Tram Trail. Running out to a wild and wolly switchback, the 'hidden segment' continues in the woods where old blue blazes mark the way. A short spin down the forest road links to the 'unnamed' trail that climbs around Round Knob. Old woods roads lead to the aptly named Stony Gap Trail. The gap here is quite stony and you'll soon find out as sections of 'ruff' trail prevail. A spin back to the Old Tram Trail retraces the ride to the switchback on Sand Mountain. Climbing over Sand Mountain the ride follows the mellow forestry road downhill to the trailhead.

THE RIDE...

0.0 From the trailhead, turn right on Sand Mountain Road, following it straight as the road surface changes to hardpacked dirt.

0.5 Turn left on to a dirt road that passes Boiling Spring Camp on the right and soon after passes around a gate.

0.7 Pass under the powerline as the trail bends left. Soon the trail will pass a small right spur that leads to the Boiling Spring enclosure. Check it out if you have time!

1.0 After climbing the steep hill and passing around a gate, bear right to find the Old Tram Trail marked by the wooden forestry signs. Turn right on the Old Tram Trail.

1.4 Pass the Rocky Corner Trail.

2.0 Cross the Cracker Bridge Trail

3.4 At the right-hand switchback, continue straight on the continuation of the Old Tram Trail. Once on the trail, blue blazes may become apparent on the trees.

4.2 Turn left on Cooper Mill Road

4.7 Turn right on the **obscure unnamed red-blazed trail** (Pirate Tr.?) and begin a sincletrack climb. If you come to the intersection of Spruce Run and Cooper Mill Roads, you missed the turn!

5.3 The trail comes out to a small clearing. Follow the right edge and turn right on the dirt woods road. *An option to shave some time would be to find the unmarked singletrack on the upper left-edge where woods road heads north. This singletrack joins with the Stony Gap Trail, see the map.

5.5 Turn left on to the Spring Mountain Trail (woods road) and travel a short way to the Stony Gap Trail (mile 5.6). Turn left on the Stony Gap Trail, following the blazes.

6.6 Pass the Stony Gap cabin and around a gate. Turn left on Spruce Run Road. Check out the cool old tram-truck wheel cemented in the cabin's moss-covered yard!

7.4 Keep left at the road fork climbing on Cooper Mill Road.

8.0 Turn right and reenter the Old Tram Trail.

8.7 Come out to the switchback on the Old Tram Trail from mile 3.4. Turn left, climbing the old, rocky tram grade.

9.4 After a series of twists and turns, turn right on Sand Mountain Road.

11.8 Turn left into the trailhead.

Watch those stream crossings! The 'Natives' can get real nasty! (yeah...thats' a 2.4" tire!)

27 ROUND KNOB TO STONY GAP

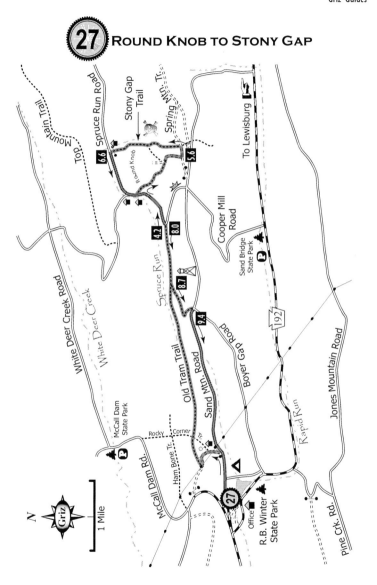

MAGS PATH TO BLACK GAP
RIDE 28

Trailhead: **McCall Dam State Park**, 21 miles from Lewisburg. From Lewisburg travel west on State Highway 192 for 18 miles. After passing Halfway Lake on the right and R.B. Winter State Park office on the left, the road will come to a unique 4-way intersection. Turn right (not hard right) on to McCall Dam Road which climbs sharply up to the Halfway Lake overlook. Follow McCall Dam Road for 3 miles to the McCall Dam State Park and park in the large lot on the right. The ride begins from this lot.

GPS: N41-1.056' W77-10.776'

Distance: 11.7 mile loop

Time: 1-3 hours

Highlights: 3 stellar old tram grades, lots 'o awesome singletrack, the "Mystery Trail", serene beauty of McCall Dam State Park and close to R.B. Winter State Park amenities.

Technical Difficulty: 4. The singletracks along this route not only offer a great cross-section of the more advanced riding in the region, but also a lesson on the local geology! Tons of broken limestone, sandstone and dolomite rock forms the beds of these old tram trails. The result are sections of trail that at first glance appear unrideable, but by keeping the front end light and staying on the 'gas' will help 'float' you through these loose, big blocks.

Aerobic Difficulty: Moderate. The ride spikes on three separate ridges, offering a significant amount of vertical gain. The flat sections, due to their rocky and technical nature, require lots of energy to push through and the forest roads offer a change of terrain, linking one great section to another.

Vertical: 1,693 feet of climbing

Climbing Distance: 6.7 miles

Maps: DCNR Bald Eagle State Forest Public Use Map.

Land Status: DCNR Bald Eagle State Forest

Ride Notes: This ride is a true 'step back into time' and destined to be a classic. Covering three of the areas most beautiful tram grades, it offers a formidable challenge along historic pathways that form the foundation of the ride. Although never built with an intention to become stellar mountain bike trails, the tram grades on this ride offer some of the finest riding in the region. Getting warmed up on the dirt road, you soon seek out the first singletrack section just before Engle Road. Finding this unnamed and unmarked "Mystery Trail" is not terribly difficult, but this one is a forgotten and hidden jewel indeed. A gradual climb crests the hill to a spectacular descent.

Linking a few short sections of forestry road leads to another unmarked but obvious trail, the Mags Path. This long-time 4-wheel drive road has been blocked to vehicles, but has always been a great mountain bike climb. Crossing the powerline and higher up, the Heintz Trail, the evidence of the old tram trail shows through as a skinny singletrack. Cresting the ridge, a rocky ride ensues, as the trail drops a wicked 370 feet in less than half a mile. Looping around to yet another old tram trail, the Black Gap Trail starts out with a burly little climb before sending you through rock garden railroad grades. The finale is a killer stretch of singletrack named after the White Deer Creek it chases back to the trailhead.

THE RIDE...

0.0 From the McCall Dam State Park Picnic Area trailhead, ride north on McCall Dam Road, passing White Deer Creek Road on the right.

1.2 Pass the Horse Path Trail.

1.8 Turn right on the unblazed "Mystery Trail", which is marked by a grassy pull-out and two large road-blocking boulders. If you arrive at an intersection with Engle Road, you missed the turn by 300 yards. The trail continues to be maintained although forestry has omitted this trail from the public use map. Enjoy this short but classic singletrack section!

2.5 Turn left on to Breon Road.

2.7 Turn left on McCall Dam Road. Soon after (mile 2.9) turn right on to Swenks Road.

3.4 Turn left on the Mags Path at a large grassy pull-out, passing around a road-blocking 'moat' and series of large boulders, continuing on an old woods road. Soon after cross a powerline (mile 3.7) and continues to climb on the other side.

4.1 Cross the Heintz Trail and continue to climb on the incredible remains of an old Wildcat tram grade. Enjoy the rocky and technical descent that lies ahead!

4.6 Turn right on to Engle Road.

6.1 After passing the Birch Still Camp on the right, turn left on to the red-blazed Black Gap Trail, as it ascends a hemlock hollow.

6.8 Cross a grassy woods road diagonally right, continuing on the Black Gap Trail. The trail will soon show evidence of the old tram grade.

9.1 Turn left on to Black Gap Road.

9.8 After crossing a

Dave riding out the classic
Wildcat grade on the Mags Trail

bridge over White Deer Creek, turn right on to the White Deer Creek Trail, located at the bend in the road and marked by a wooden forestry sign.

11.7 Turn right on to McCall Dam Road, arriving at the trailhead.

28 MAGS PATH TO BLACK GAP

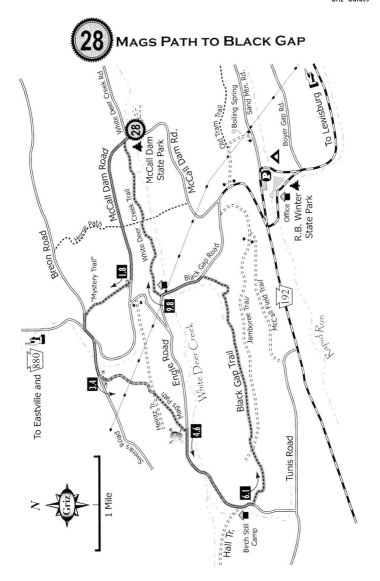

HEINTZ TRAIL TO SWENKS GAP
RIDE 29

Trailhead: **McCall Dam State Park,** 21 miles from Lewisburg. From Lewisburg travel west on State Highway 192 for 18 miles. After passing Halfway Lake on the right and R.B. Winter State Park office on the left, the road will come to a unique 4-way intersection. Turn right (not hard right) on to McCall Dam Road which climbs sharply up to the Halfway Lake overlook. Follow McCall Dam Road for 3 miles to the McCall Dam State Park and park in the large lot on the right. The ride begins from this lot.

GPS: N41-1.056' W77-10.776'

Distance: 7.8 mile loop

Time: 1-2 hours

Highlights: Excellent novice loop, beautiful trail, small overlooks, spectacular trailhead location and it's close to R.B. Winter State Park amenities.

Technical Difficulty: 1. Following old woods roads and forestry roads, there are very few obstacles along this ride. The obstacles on the trail can easily be avoided, as the paths are wide enough to accommodate 2-riders wide.

Aerobic Difficulty: Easy. What a great outing for budding mountain bike riders. A loop short enough to get through in a small amount of time, yet offers some great trail that warrants knobby tires. The climbs are on an easy grade and the descents are truly exciting.

Vertical: 891 feet of climbing

Climbing Distance: 3.9 miles

Maps: DCNR Bald Eagle State Forest Public Use Map.

Land Status: DCNR Bald Eagle State Forest

Ride Notes: An outstanding cruise for those novice riders looking for a taste of mountain biking without suffering through the typical rocky and brutal terrain of the region. I give this ride the "Triple-S" rating; Short, Sweet and Smooth! Beginning at the beautiful trailhead location, the ride warms up on well-maintained forestry

29 HEINTZ TRAIL TO SWENKS GAP

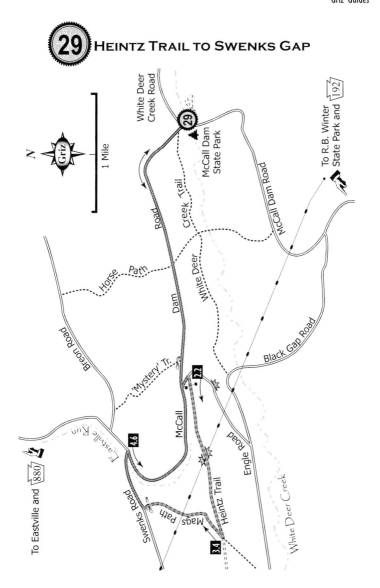

road. Two quick turns take you from McCall Dam Road to the Heintz Trail, which rolls out along a dividing ridge. Along the way the rider is treated to a small double-vista at a powerline crossing with a chance to see a Red-tailed hawk. The ride heads deeper into the woods and turns on to the remains of an old logging grade, the Mags Path. This wide path gently sweeps down into the Swenks Gap area, passing under the powerline a second time. A short and rough 4-wheel drive section empties on Swenks Gap Road, which begins another mellow climb back to the trailhead. Turning on to McCall Dam Road, the final stretch climbs a bit more before a smooth descent to the picnic area trailhead. Now get out that picnic lunch or fly rod and enjoy the pristine surroundings!

THE RIDE...

0.0 From the McCall Dam State Park Picnic Area trailhead, ride north on McCall Dam Road, passing White Deer Creek Road on the right.

1.2 Pass the Horse Path Trail.

2.1 Turn left on to Engle Road. Soon after (mile2.2) turn right on to the Heintz Trail woods road.

2.8 Cross under the powerline. Check out the views, especially looking northwest, where the trail will cross this powerline again.

3.4 At a 4-way intersection (may only appear as a right spur woods road), turn right on to the Mags Path, a grassy woods road.

3.8 Cross under the powerline again and continue on the opposite side.

4.1 Turn right on to Swenks Road.

4.6 Turn right on to McCall Dam Road and follow it back to the trailhead.

5.7 Pass Engle Road on the right.

7.8 Arrive back at the trailhead.

Spike Buck to Top Mountain
Ride 30

Trailhead: **McCall Dam State Park,** 21 miles from Lewisburg. From Lewisburg travel west on State Highway 192 for 18 miles. After passing Halfway Lake on the right and R.B. Winter State Park office on the left, the road will come to a unique 4-way intersection. Turn right (not hard right) on to McCall Dam Road which climbs sharply up to the Halfway Lake overlook. Follow McCall Dam Road for 3 miles to the McCall Dam State Park and park in the large lot on the right. The ride begins from this lot.

GPS: N41-1.056' W77-10.776'

Distance: 26.0 mile loop

Time: 3-6 hours

Highlights: Historic old tram grades, awesome scenery and great singletrack with rocks, rocks and more rocks!

Technical Difficulty: 5. The route covers some of the rockiest trail sections in the northeast section of Bald Eagle State Forest. Most of the singletrack trail sections are littered with sustained sections of rocks that will keep even the most experienced rider on the edge of their seat!

Aerobic Difficulty: Strenuous. Lots of climbing, descending and lots of flat riding through tough terrain. This ride is stout in every sense of the word, are you up for the challenge?

Vertical: 3,243 feet of climbing

Climbing Distance: 13.6 miles

Maps: DCNR Bald Eagle State Forest Public Use Map.

Land Status: DCNR Bald Eagle State Forest

Ride Notes: A rugged ride for stone-lovin' cowboys on steel steeds! The ride covers many old tram grades, most of which are very rocky in nature. The ride begins in one of the most beautiful places in the Northern Bald Eagle State Forest, the McCall Dam State Park Picnic Area. From this awesome trailhead, a warm-up on forestry roads leads to the sometimes-marked Stony Hollow Trail. Although not difficult to find, the trail was not proposed as one that forestry would continue to maintain but has been adopted by others and myself. Stony Hollow empties on another forestry road, which parallels and then crosses Interstate 80. A bit more riding on forestry roads, has you wondering where all the rocks are… just you wait! The Spike Buck Trail dives down an old tram trail into a dank hollow where the Kurtz Gap Trail switchbacks left, climbing on yet another old rail grade. Crossing Pine Flat Road, the old tram grade continues on the flat but rocky Red Tongue Trail 4-wheel drive road and out to a five-point intersection. The Mile Run Trail drops down the drainage for which it was named and follows an extremely rocky old tram grade. Back out on another forestry road, Mile Run Road crosses under Interstate 80 at an interchange and the ride takes on another climb connecting White Deer Pike, White Deer Creek and Running Gap Roads. The kicker comes with the 5 mile rock-fest atop the rugged Top Mountain Trail which will have your body feelin' as flogged as a Florida palm tree after the hurricane season! Forestry roads return your weary ass to the trailhead and by now you've probably had enough of the bony ridges of Bald Eagle.

THE RIDE…

0.0 From the trailhead lot, ride north on McCall Dam Road and turn right on to White Deer Creek Road.

0.8 Turn left, climbing Garden Hollow Road.

2.0 Turn right on to the Stony Hollow Trail. The Stony Hollow Trail may be blazed, but if not it is marked by a pair of large boulders at a narrow grassy inset.

3.7 Turn right on to Garden Hollow Road.

4.1 Turn left on to the paved White Deer Pike and ride the bridge across Interstate 80. Once across the bridge turn right on to Zimmerman Road (mile 4.3).

30 SPIKE BUCK TO TOP MOUNTAIN

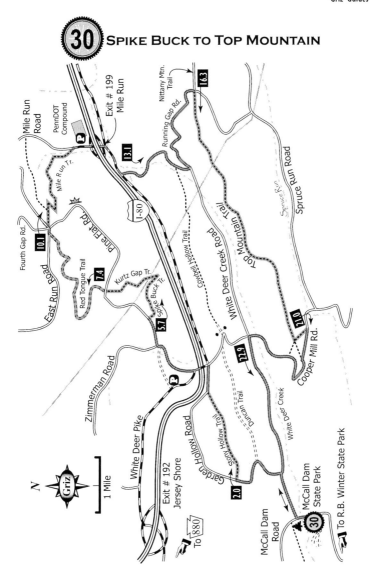

157

5.1 Turn right on to Pine Flat Road.

5.7 Turn right on the Spike Buck Trail. At the bottom of the drainage the trail will switchback hard left and becomes the Kurtz Gap Trail.

7.4 Cross Pine Flat Road and continue on the marked Red Tongue Trail, a 4-wheel drive road.

10.1 Turn right on East Run Road and come to a 4-way intersection. Ride across the intersection, picking up the red-blazed Mile Run Trail. As you descend, the trail will pass a left-spur red-blazed trail, continue straight. Soon after the trail will turn on a series of switchbacks. The trail gets rough down low so saddle up.

11.9 Cross Mile Run Creek and turn right on Mile Run Road. The road will turn paved and pass under both lanes of Interstate 80 (mile 12.3) at Exit #199, Mile Run.

12.5 Turn right at the T intersection on White Deer Pike.

13.1 Turn left on White Deer Creek Road.

14.6 Turn hard left on Running Gap Road.

16.3 At the crest of Nittany Mountain, turn right on to the Top Mountain Trail, grunting and grinding your way across the ridge.

20.8 Keep left at a fork marked by a grassy campsite complete with fire ring and ride over a dirt berm. The trail becomes a wide singletrack as it descends.

21.0 Turn right on Coopers Mill Road, climbing back over Nittany Mountain.

22.9 Turn left on to White Deer Creek Road.

26.0 Turn left on McCall Dam Road to the trailhead.

Joe ridge riding the Top Mountain Trail

DYNAMITE SHACK
RIDE 31

Trailhead: **White Deer Pike trailhead**, East of Exit 192 off of I-80, 23 miles from Milton. From Milton travel west on Interstate 80 to Exit #192, Jersey Shore. At the end of the exit ramp, turn right on to White Deer Pike. Travel for 2.5 miles to a large parking area on the left, surrounded by tall pine trees. Turn left into this parking area and the ride begins from here. If you should come to a bridge that passes over Interstate 80, you missed the trailhead lot.

GPS: N41-2.772' W77-8.593'

Distance: 13.3 mile loop

Time: 1-3 hours

Highlights: Historic old tram grades, the Dynamite Shack, awesome scenery, great singletrack and options to customize the ride for length and technical difficulty.

Technical Difficulty: 3. The toughest parts of the route can be found along the Buck Gap and bottom of the Kurtz Gap Trails, which are rated **4+.**

Aerobic Difficulty: Moderate. The ride begins with almost 5 miles of climbing, mainly on smooth forest road. The singletrack sections are challenging enough to demand some energy, even on a downhill grade. By cutting out the Kurtz Gap and/or the Buck Gap sections, the ride become significantly easier.

Vertical: 1,764 feet of climbing

Climbing Distance: 6.2 miles

Maps: DCNR Bald Eagle State Forest and Tiadaghton State Forest Public Use Maps.

Land Status: DCNR Bald Eagle State Forest and Tiadaghton State Forest

Ride Notes: The Dynamite Shack is one diverse ride that covers everything from smooth forest roads, stony old tram grades, grassy pipeline cuts and rocky singletracks. The ride reminds me of a great brew, it's smooth at first then leaches a bit of savory flavor to finish with a robust kick. Yes, tasty indeed it may have you going back for a second round but don't let me twist your arm, after all you hafta drive home! Looking at the map, the ride is broken up into three basic sections; the Kurtz Gap, Pine Flat and main loop section. You have the option to pedal only parts of the ride using the detailed map to link your own custom ride. The description that follows is an account of the entire ride. The ride begins with a good warp-up past the Dynamite Shack, climbing to Pine Flat Road. Along the way up, an awesome side trail option into Kurtz Gap will please any adventurous rider who dares to run this short spur along old tram grades. The ride continues to climb around Pine Flat and turns on the old Red Tongue Trail tram grade. Back out on Pine Flat Road, a few miles of forest road drops you on the Buck Gap Trail where a tuff n' technical descent awaits. The final leg runs an old ATV style trail through a timber cut, before cruising back on the paved road to the trailhead. ***Note:** *This ride has been rerouted due the sensitive nature of the pipeline trail and it's proximity to the Mohn Mill Ponds Wild Plant Sanctuary. The old route has been shown only to alert past users of the new route. Please follow the new route.*

THE RIDE...

0.0 From the trailhead lot, begin the ride in the northwest corner of the lot on a dirt doubletrack. The trail will soon pass a cabin and not long after passes the Dynamite Shack on the right.

0.9 Turn left on Zimmerman Road and soon after turn right on Pine Flat Road.

1.4 Turn right on the Spike Buck Trail.

2.2 The Spike Buck trail switchbacks hard left on to the Kurtz Gap Trail in the bottom of Kurtz Gap.

3.1 Turn right on Pine Flat Road and continue to climb.

5.5 Come to the 4-way intersection with Pine Flat, Mile Run and East Run Roads. Turn left on East Run Road and immediately after

160

31 DYNAMITE SHACK

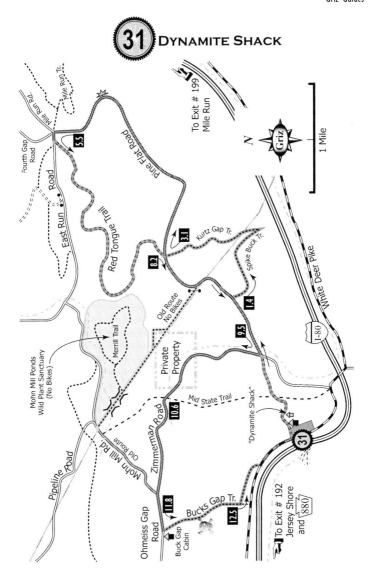

turn left on the Red Tongue Trail signed as a "Driveable Trail".

8.2 Turn right on Pine Flat Road.

8.7 Pass the gated pipeline cut (this is where the old route turned).

9.5 Turn right on Zimmerman Road. Pass the Mid State Trail (mile 10.6).

11.5 Continue straight on Ohmeiss Gap Road at the intersection with Mohn Mill Road.

11.8 Turn left just before the Buck Gap Cabin on the Buck Gap Trail. Enjoy the steep, rocky descent

12.5 Turn left on the old woods road, just before the trail exits on White Deer Pike.

12.7 After crossing under a powerline, turn right and follow the ATV trail out to White Deer Pike. Turn left on the paved road.

13.3 Turn left into the trailhead lot.

Karl feeling the 'heat' at the Dynamite Shack

Jay, making his 2nd guidebook appearence...
doing what he does best...recycling ride maps.

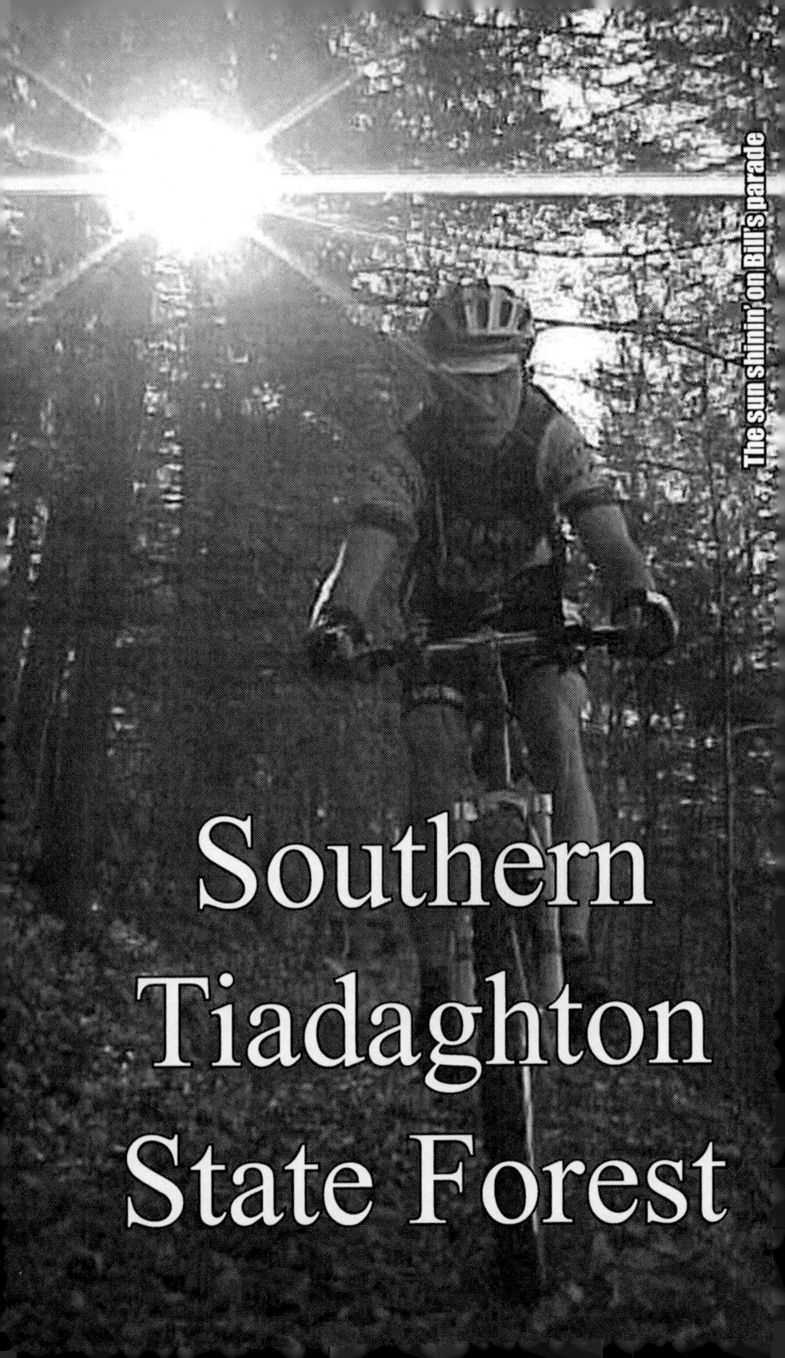

Southern
Tiadaghton
State Forest

The sun shinin' on Bill's parade

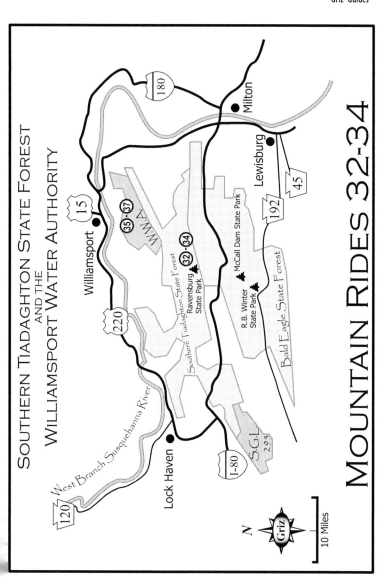

SOUTHERN TIADAGHTON STATE FOREST
AND THE
WILLIAMSPORT WATER AUTHORITY

MOUNTAIN RIDES 32-34

SOUTHERN TIADAGHTON TOUR
RIDE 32

Trailhead: Klabfleish Road atop Ravensburg State Park, 23 miles from Milton. From Milton travel west on Interstate 80 to Exit #192, Jersey Shore. At the end of the exit ramp, turn left passing the gas station and travel to the junction of State Highway 880. Turn right on to State Highway 880 following it north for 4 miles, towards Ravensburg State Park. Turn right on to a dirt forestry road, Sand Spring Road, and climb to a 4-way intersection. Turn right at the 4-way intersection on to Kalbfleish Road. Travel along Kalbfleish for 0.3 miles, parking in the large gravel pullout on the left. If you come to Ravensburg State Park, you missed the turn up Sand Spring Road. **GPS**: N41-5.669' W77-13.316'

Distance: 31.9 mile loop.

Time: 6-9 hours

Highlights: Massive loop of epic proportions, rugged trail and tough terrain, mid-ride spring, incredible sections of singletrack, Castle Rock, Ravensburg State Park amenities.

Technical Difficulty: **4**. Although interspersed well with forest roads and old woods roads, this trail demands a high level of fitness and skill to prevent a night out in the woods. Sections of new singletrack will need years to become smoother and gnarly rock gardens will still prevail in some locations.

Aerobic Difficulty: **Strenuous**. Gotta be on the gas to get this one done in a day! Loads of miles and even more climbing is the name of the game. Get an early start!

Vertical: 4,268 feet of climbing

Climbing Distance: 15.6 miles

Maps: DCNR Bald Eagle State Forest and Tiadaghton Public Use Maps

Land Status: DCNR Bald Eagle and Tiadaghton State Forests

Ride Notes: This ride is of epic proportions and not to be taken lightly. Over 4,000 feet of tough climbing and even tougher trail surfaces, this route is for folks who don't mind suffering a wee-bit. There are a few life-saving springs along the way, but I can't say how safe they are. The spring found around mid-ride is probably the safest, but don't take my work for it, pack filtration. The route is rough n' tough and gets a bit rowdy in places. Make sure you're in a good mindset to slog out the entire loop or reference the maps for a custom loop and/or possible bail-out points. The entire loop follows red-blazes and the following descriptions will help you stay on route.

The ride begins on Sand Spring Flat just above the rocky canyon walls of Ravensburg State Park. From here the ride embarks on the daunting journey in a clockwise direction. A short loop around Sand Spring Flat will give you the abbreviated version of the bigger loop. If you find that 25+ more miles of just the same will be too much for you, bail out at the 4-mile mark, right at the trailhead. From this point on you travel further and further from your vehicle, be prepared as the road ahead is rough! Linking fresh-cut trail with old

singletrack and woods roads, the ride progresses out Fourth Gap Road and the pictured *mid-ride spring*. Plenty more climbing follows as the route works up through Fourth, Third and Second Gaps to a loop above Lick Run.

A wild stretch of dual-sport trail cuts out above Mile Run and continues to work westward. The ride turns north, crosses Pipeline Road and climbs again on a long stretch of poorly maintained forest roads. The final highlight comes with the stellar screamer descent on the Mountain Gap Trail, an old log slide, as the route spins back to the trailhead.

THE RIDE...

0.0 From the parking area trailhead pull-out, head back out Kalbfleish Road to the intersection with Sand Spring Road.

0.2 Cross the intersection and continue on the gated woods road. You will soon pass a large wooden routered cross-country ski trail sign on the right.

0.5 Pass a blue blazed left spur trail. Soon after (mile 0.7) keep left at a fork heading into the woods at an old wooden 4x4 signpost.

1.5 Turn left on the grassy woods road and follow it past another old footpath that drops down left into the State Park. Soon after the trail will bend right and run along the ridge top, passing another left-spur trail.

2.0 The trail turns 90-degrees right and follows the State Forest boundary. Soon after (mile 2.1) the trail breaks off 90-degrees left on to a tight, rocky singletrack.

2.5 The singletrack turns 90 degrees right on to another singletrack that gets better. Soon this singletrack will become a woods road at mile 3.0.

3.2 Cross Sand Spring Road and continue on the gated woods road.

3.7 Turn left on an old woods road that descends, looking carefully for the red blazes. The old road grade bends left and follows an old logging railroad grade for about 30 yards. The trail then switchbacks hard right and crosses a wooden bridge. Did ya feel the old railroad ties under your tire? Once across the bridge, the trail will soon branch left.

4.0 Turn left on a wide grassy woods road. **If you don't think you're up for the rest, bail-out by turning right on to a wide grassy woods road and cross the dirt mound to the trailhead lot on Kalbfleish Road.

4.5 Turn right as the trail breaks off right climbing a rugged section that leads through the woods to the Sawalt Trail woods road. Soon after (mile 4.7) turn left on to the Sawalt Trail. Pass a pipeline cut at mile 5.3.

(32) SOUTHERN TIADAGHTON TOUR

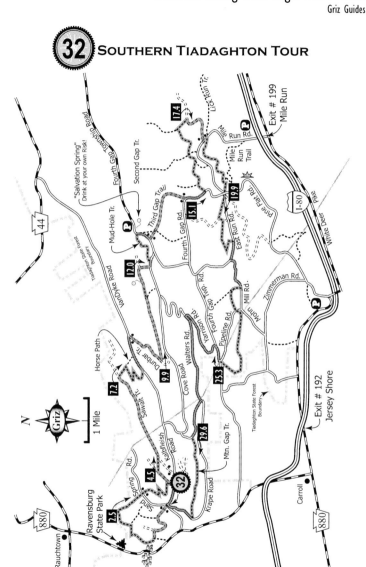

7.2 After passing through a large clearing with left-spurring woods roads, turn right on to the Horse Path Trail at a wooden signpost stating the trail junction. It gets kinda steep up higher so you will need to bike-hike the rest of the way. Soon the trail will turn right (mile 7.5) on to a newer logging road/trail which switchbacks up to Vandyke Road.

8.2 Turn left on Vandyke Road.

9.0 Turn right on the gated Dunbar Trail woods road, marked by the wooden sign, and descend.

9.9 Lay on the brakes! Turn hard left on to another grassy woods road, passing around some boulders. You will soon pass the old Mid State Trail.

11.4 Come to the end of the woods road. There are two trails that lead off from here, take the red blazed trail straight (left) into the woods on rough trail which soon connects with another grassy woods road. The right spur trail is the West Refuge Trail, which comes out to Cove Road, another bailout point! You will pass an old spring pouring from a rusted pipe at mile11.8, it looks kinda rough but in a pinch it might do?!

12.0 Turn right at a T intersection, descending the woods road. Cross the pictured *sketchy log bridge* over White Deer Hole Creek (mile 12.3) and turn left on to Cove Road. Soon after turn left onto a wide singletrack at mile 12.5, keep alert!

13.2 The trail dumps out on to the paved Fourth Gap Road. Turn right on Fourth

Gap Road. Ignore the red blazes as they break off left on to the Metzger Trail and continue up the road a bit to the Third Gap Road, a gated woods road on the left. Turn left up Third Gap Road (mile 13.5) and soon the red blazes will rejoin the route at the intersection of the Metzger Trail. Continue climbing Third Gap Road. ***A water tank-up (The "Salvation Spring" see picture..) is located just 100 yards down on the left, from this mile point, at a large clearing with a concrete slab. Flowing from a pipe is pure (?) spring water, so cool off, tank-up and drink if you dare. This location is nearing the mid-point of the ride.***

15.1 After passing around a gate turn left on to Fourth Gap Road. After riding a short way (mile 15.5), turn left at a grassy pull-out on to a woodsy doubletrack that soon turns to a singletrack.

15.8 Merge right on to a grassy woods road.

16.4 Turn left at the T intersection and descend. Check out the small view on the left, out over the Shoemaker Knob and Potato Hill. You'll pass a triangle shaped left spur.

17.2 Turn right at a T intersection, climbing the steep hill on an ATV trail. At the top of the hill turn right at the T intersection (mile 17.4) on to a woods road and ride out along the ridge.

18.3 After passing around a gate, turn left on to Mile Run Road and descend a short way. Soon the trail turns right (mile 18.4) at a dirt pull-out, and crosses over a dirt mound continuing on a singletrack trail. You will also have passed the Lick Run Trail on the left. Enjoy the tight singletrack with sporadic views out over the Mile Run drainage.

19.6 Turn right on to the Mile Run/Lake Trail. Come out to a 4-way intersection with Mile Run, Fourth Gap and Pine Flat and East Run Roads at mile 19.9. Ride out straight on East Run Road.

20.0 Turn right on the red-blazed singletrack.

20.5 Turn left at the T intersection on to the Metzger Trail woods road. Soon after turn right on the old woods road.

21.5 After the trail switchbacks left, it will bend right and come out to East Run Road. Turn right on East Run Road.

22.0 Turn left at the T intersection on Mohn Mill Road.

22.8 Turn right on the Brushy Ridge Trail, climbing.

23.4 Cross Pipeline Road and soon after cross a pipeline cut.

24.8 The trail turns 90 degrees right as it follows the forestry boundary. Soon after keep right at the fork.

25.3 Come out to the intersection of Pipeline and Fourth Gap Roads. Turn right on Fourth Gap Road.

25.6 Turn left on Yarrison Road.

26.8 Turn left at the T on Walters Road.

28.7 Turn right at the T on Krape Road.

29.6 Turn left on the red-blazed Mountain Gap Trail and climb. Get ready to enjoy the ride!

31.5 Turn right on Krape Road.

32.0 Turn right on Sand Spring Road then an immediate right on Kalbfleish Road

32.2 Arrive at the trailhead.

Share the Trails!

Sand Spring Flat
Ride 33

Trailhead: **Klabfleish Road atop Ravensburg State Park**, 23 miles from Milton. From Milton travel west on Interstate 80 to Exit #192, Jersey Shore. At the end of the exit ramp, turn left passing the gas station and travel to the junction of State Highway 880. Turn right on to State Highway 880 following it north for 4 miles, towards Ravensburg State Park. Turn right on to a dirt forestry road, Sand Spring Road, and climb to a 4-way intersection. Turn right at the 4-way intersection on to Kalbfleish Road. Travel along Kalbfleish for 0.3 miles, parking in the large gravel pullout on the left. If you come to Ravensburg State Park, you missed the turn up Sand Spring Road. **GPS**: N41-5.669' W77-13.316'

Distance: 4.1 mile loop

Time: 30 minuets to 1 ½ hours.

Highlights: Short loop with a fun section of rugged trail, little climbing involved, deep-woods feel, historic old logging railroad grade, Ravensburg State Park, Castle Rocks, options to extend the ride with the *Mountain Gap Trail, Ride # 34.*

Technical Difficulty: 3+. A bit burly in sections, this short but stout loop covers a variety of terrain. The second half of the ride holds the toughest stuff, with new sections of fresh-cut trail that run along the steep edge of the ridge and Tiadaghton State Forest boundary.

Aerobic Difficulty: Moderate. The ride runs around the Sand Spring Flat atop the ridge. With little change in elevation major hill climbs aren't an issue on this ride. The hardest part will be pedaling through the rough sections of new trail, which are primitive and rocky in nature.

Vertical: 797 feet of climbing

Climbing Distance: 2.4 miles

Maps: DCNR Bald Eagle State Forest Public Use Map.

Land Status: DCNR Bald Eagle State Forest

Southern Tiadaghton State Forest

Ride Notes: Located high atop the deep slotted canyon of Ravensburg State Park, this ride rambles along the rolling Sand Spring Flat ridge top. The nearby attractions make this a great destination. Fishing, hiking and rock climbing are just a few things you can do before or after the ride. Ravensburg State Park is a beautiful and somewhat tranquil place to hang out and have a picnic. Although State Highway 880 cuts through the heart of the park, the rugged nature of the landscape somehow distracts your attention from the road noise. The ride is merely a small section of the *Southern Tiadaghton Tour (Ride #31)* of the Central Mountain Trail system and is blazed red throughout the route. Mid-State Trail hikers of the Keystone Trail Association were cryin' over the fact that the CMT was run on a small section of logging road that is also part of the MST . Sorry guys! If it weren't for the loggers' way back when, you wouldn't have much of a trail to hike on.

Beginning at the large parking area trailhead, the ride swings back to the 4-way intersection and hooks up on a gated woods road. Now be kind to any overly sensitive hiker you might run into, you might be ruining their woodland experience, but feel free to let them know if they are ruining your mountain biking experience. Not long after the gate, a large wooden sign states the cross-country ski trail system that lies ahead. The ride climbs a bit passing a cool side trail that drops steeply into a draw and climbs right back out. As the route follows the contour of the flat, it turns right at an intersection of the Mid-State Trail. The trail runs the western rim of the flat before turning sharply at the forest boundary. A second sharp turn has you continuing on the fresh-cut trail that gets a bit rough and rocky in places. At the high-point of 1,878 feet, the route takes another sharp turn and morphs from singletrack to doubletrack grassy woods road. Across Sand Spring Road the ride follows more grassy trail, descending to an old railroad grade. A very short stint along this ancient grade leads to a newly built bridge and a climb back to the trailhead.

33 SAND SPRING FLAT

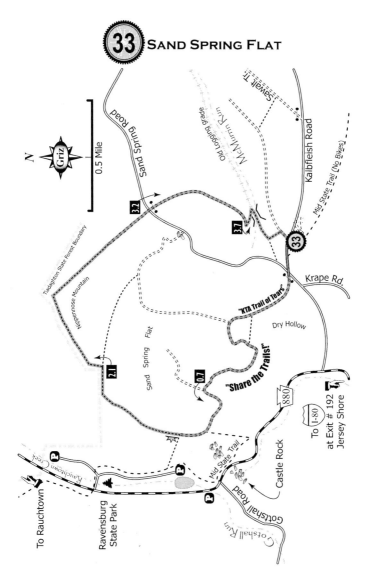

N

Griz

0.5 Mile

Sand Spring Road

Sawall Tr.

Kalbfleish Road

Old Logging grade

McMurrIn Run

Mid State Trail (No Bikes)

3.2

3.7

33

Tiadaghton State Forest Boundary

Nippennose Mountain

Krape Rd.

Dry Hollow

"KTA Trail of Tears"

Sand Spring Flat

0.7

"Share the Trails!"

2.1

To Rauchtown

Rauchtown Creek

Ravensburg State Park

Mid State Trail

Castle Rock

880

To I-80 at Exit # 192 Jersey Shore

Gotshall Road

Gotshall Run

THE RIDE...

0.0 From the parking area trailhead pull-out head back out Kalbfleish Road to the intersection with Sand Spring Road.

0.2 Cross the intersection and continue on the gated woods road. You will soon pass a large wooden routered cross-country ski trail sign on the right.

0.5 Pass a blue blazed left spur trail.

0.7 Keep left at a fork heading into the woods at an old wooden 4x4 signpost.

1.5 Turn left on the grassy woods road and follow it past another old footpath that drops down left into the State Park. Soon after the trail will bend right and run along the ridge top, leaving the MST to descend to Ravensburg State Park.

2.0 The trail turns 90 degrees right and follows the State Forest boundary. Soon after (mile 2.1) the trail breaks off 90 degrees left on to a tight, rocky singletrack into the woods.

2.5 The singletrack turns 90 degrees right on to another singletrack that gets better. Soon this singletrack will become a woods road at mile 3.0.

3.2 Cross Sand Spring Road and continue on the gated woods road.

3.7 Turn left on an old woods road that descends, looking carefully for the red blazes. The old road grade bends left and follows an old logging railroad grade for about 30 yards. The trail then switchbacks hard right and crosses a wooden bridge. Did ya feel the old railroad ties under your tire? Once across the bridge, the trail will soon branch left.

4.1 Turn right on a wide grassy woods road and cross the dirt mound to the trailhead lot on Kalbfleish Road.

MOUNTAIN GAP TRAIL
RIDE 34

Trailhead: **Klabfleish Road atop Ravensburg State Park**, 23 miles from Milton. From Milton travel west on Interstate 80 to Exit #192, Jersey Shore. At the end of the exit ramp, turn left passing the gas station and travel to the junction of State Highway 880. Turn right on to State Highway 880 following it north for 4 miles, towards Ravensburg State Park. Turn right on to a dirt forestry road, Sand Spring Road, and climb to a 4-way intersection. Turn right at the 4-way intersection on to Kalbfleish Road. Travel along Kalbfleish for 0.3 miles, parking in the large gravel pullout on the left. If you come to Ravensburg State Park, you missed the turn up Sand Spring Road. **GPS**: N41-5.669' W77-13.316'

Distance: 11.1 mile loop

Time: 1 ½ to 3 hours

Highlights: Classic old log-slide chute, diverse and excellent trail riding, great wildlife viewing, old logging railroad grades turned killer singletrack, can be linked with *Sand Spring Flat Ride # 33*.

Technical Difficulty: 3+. The ride is filled with great singletrack sections, many of which are fun and technical. From rocks and roots to sharp climbs and steep descents, this ride will definitely keep your interest throughout.

Aerobic Difficulty: Moderate. The ride faces two substantial climbs; the first is shorter but very steep in grade. The second climb is less steep in grade but climbs a sustained 900 vertical feet. The climbs aren't the only physical challenge, the singletrack sections demand some 'gas' as well.

Vertical: 1,693 feet of climbing

Climbing Distance: 5.9 miles

Maps: DCNR Bald Eagle State Forest Public Use Map.

Land Status: DCNR Bald Eagle State Forest

Ride Notes: Named after the Mountain Gap Trail section found at the end of the ride, this trail highlight follows a rich piece of woodland logging history, an old log slide. Log slides were built in places where it was too steep or ineffective to build a railroad grade. Pairs of logs were spiked together in parallel fashion and where they met, a 'V' shape was carved. Timbered logs were then rolled onto the log slide and skidded or slid down the mountain on these wooden slides. The 'bellied' grade stands as a reminder of a time long ago. The ride is merely a small section of the *Southern Tiadaghton Tour (Ride #32)* of the Central Mountain Trail system and is blazed red throughout most of the route.

Starting at the trailhead, the ride has a short warm-up on grassy woods road before climbing a short, steep and rough trail to grassy Sawalt Trail. A mellow spin out along this grade offers the possible glimpse of a turkey or deer before climbing the first serious section. A tough 550-foot push up the Horse Path puts you atop North White Deer Ridge and a rewarding ripper descent down the Dunbar Trail. Cove Road is the next point of attack, climbing a sustained 700 feet to the Mountain Gap Trail where the remaining 200 feet climb to the true summit knob of North White Deer Mountain at an elevation of 2,210 feet. The trail then hooks on to the final gem, taking you back in time and throwing you down "in the slide", the same pathway taken by many timbered old-growth hemlocks. As you rip down this incredible descent, imagine the tons of timber that rocketed down this slide to the train cars waiting below. No train will be waiting for you though, as the trail empties out on to Krape Road and gently winds back to the trailhead.

THE RIDE...

0.0 From the parking area trailhead, cross around the huge pile of timber/dirt on the right side and ride out on the grassy woods road, looking for the red blazes on the right.

0.5 Turn right as the trail breaks off right climbing a rugged section that leads through the woods to the Sawalt Trail woods road.

34 MOUNTAIN GAP TRAIL

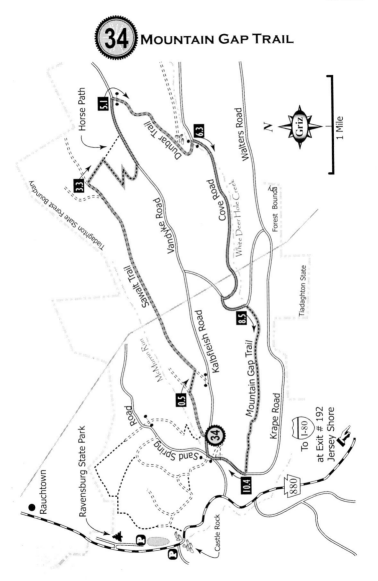

0.7 Turn left on to the Sawalt Trail.

1.4 Pass a pipeline cut.

3.3 After passing through a large clearing with left-spurring woods roads, turn right on to the Horse Path trail at a wooden sign post stating the trail junction. It gets kinda steep up higher so you will need to bike-hike the rest of the way. Soon the trail will turn right (mile 3.6) on to a newer logging road/trail which switchbacks up to Vandyke Road.

4.3 Turn left on Vandyke Road.

5.1 Turn right on the gated Dunbar Trail woods road, marked by the wooden sign, and descend.

6.3 After passing a grassy woods road on the left (mile 6.0), the woods road bends left and exits on Cove Road. Turn right on Cove Road.

8.2 Turn left on Walters Road

8.5 Turn right on the red blazed Mountain Gap Trail and get ready to have some serious singletrack fun.

10.4 Turn right on Krape Road.

10.9 Turn right on Kalbfleish Road.

11.1 Trailhead.

Moss 'ghost' bumps are all that remains of an ancient old rail grade

Top: Karl givin' Jay his 7,843 lecture on carryin' a tube
Bottom: A beautiful pair of Pennsylvania Bald Eagles

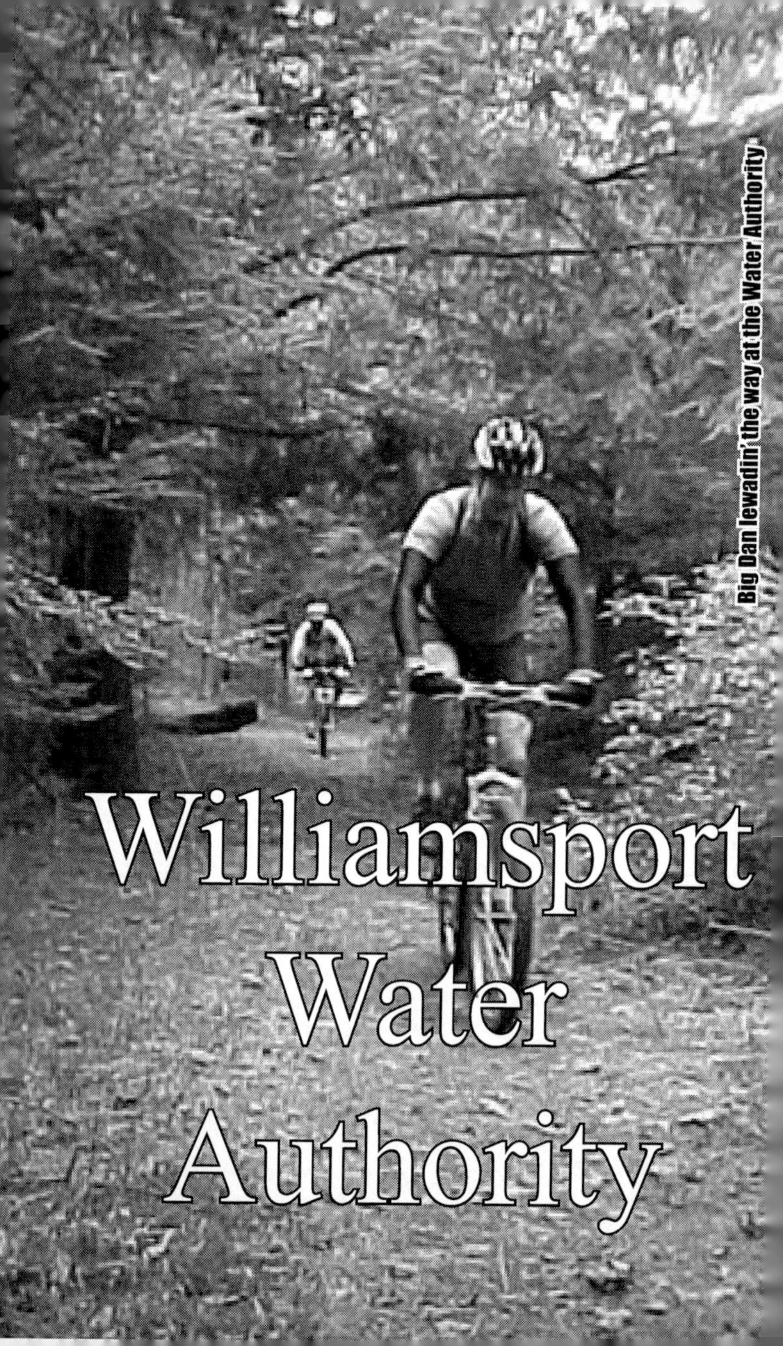

Big Dan lewadin' the way at the Water Authority.

Williamsport

Water

Authority

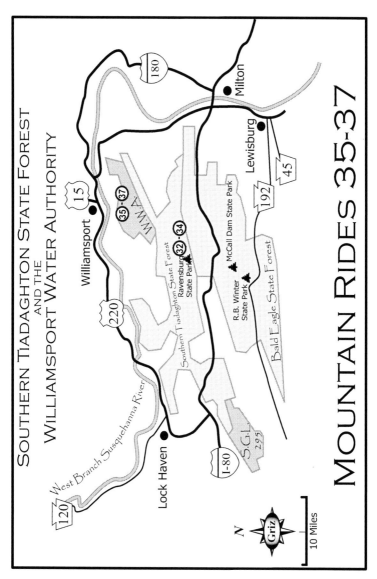

SOUTHERN TIADAGHTON STATE FOREST
AND THE
WILLIAMSPORT WATER AUTHORITY

MOUNTAIN RIDES 35-37

MOSQUITO VALLEY
RIDE 35

Trailhead: **Williamsport Water Authority Treatment Plant**, 4.5 miles from Williamsport. From Williamsport proper, cross the U.S Route 15 bridge and head into South Williamsport. Once across the bridge, turn right and follow State Highway 654 west along the river to Douboistown. In the heart of the very small town of Douboistown, turn left on to Valley Road. Valley Road is easy to miss and best identified by an Exxon Mini Market gas station on one corner and on the adjacent corner, the Valley Inn restaurant. Travel 0.6 miles along Valley Road and turn left on Mosquito Valley Road, which is also marked with a steel sign stating the 'Williamsport Water Authority'. Soon after keep left at the road fork. Take this road 1.6 miles to a dead-end turn-around, and pass through the gate into the Williamsport Water Authority. Turn right and park in the gravel parking area, denoted by the wooden sign. You must sign in at the building entrance. **GPS**: N41-11.965' W77-2.590'
Distance: 15.8 mile loop.
Time: 2-3 hours
Highlights: Excellent woods roads, historic mile-marker, numerous scattered ruins of stone walls and old farm homes, tranquil beauty of the area surrounding the Mosquito Reservoir and many options to extend or shorten the ride.
Technical Difficulty: **1**. Most of the ride follows well-maintained woods-type service roads. The roads vary from gravel to grass with most sections comprised of hardpacked dirt. The entire ride cruises mellow surfaces including the final singletrack section.
Aerobic Difficulty: **Moderate**. The ride climbs a bunch and the grades are sustained. The grassy and gravel woods roads surfaces are also a bit slow requiring an extra push to pedal through. Don't forget that all the climbs are rewarded with a downhill.
Vertical: 1,897 feet of climbing
Climbing Distance: 7.8 miles

...ımpı...ı. ııı large land
...ı, wııuı abounds with wild deer, turkey and trout.

This playground isn't only for the bears though, as a quick stroke of the pen allows access to the many miles of harpacked trails. The ride begins at the WWA Treatment Facility building where riders need to sign-in on the clipboard at the building entrance and then its around the gate and out on the trail.

The better part of the first half of the ride climbs and climbs and climbs some more. But hey! What goes up must come down, right? The first climb tackles the north face of Raccoon Mountain with a short but fun downhill. Next comes the cavernous climb to the saddle between Raccoon Mountain and White Deer Ridge.

Mosquito Reservoir

Tall, dark hemlocks and massive mossy boulders line the way as the ride peaks out on this ancient highway at a historic mile-marker. Signed and dated by the carver, this stout stone stands like a silent sentinel along a forgotten highway. Another teaser downhill leads to the final climb around the north shore of Mosquito Valley Reservoir. Old stone walls and many foundation ruins lie scattered within plain view of the trail. Careful observers will get a true sense of the farm community that once thrived in this steep and rugged valley. The western route turns east at this point and begins a predominately downhill journey. Passing some familiar terrain, the old highway leads to the finale singletrack of the Bluebird Trail. A short climb ends at the expansive Remington Estate foundation ruins. This massive structure was probably a spectacular house but now is home to a few large trees that have grown from it's dirt cellar floors. A well-deserved windy singletrack follows a fun grade as it snakes its way down to the trailhead. The ride can be tailored to a shorter length using the map and can be extended by combining with *Ride #36 Heller Reservoir* to include both reservoirs for an excellent days outing.

THE RIDE...

0.0 From the parking area, ride back out to Mosquito Valley road and turn right. Pass around a gate on the left side and continue on the dirt road.

0.5 Continue straight at a 4-way intersection on the Lower Parks Trail.

1.2 Merge left on a wood road and soon cross an old stone bridge with some backcountry humor.

2.0 Keep left at the fork soon crossing a concrete bridge at mile 2.3.

2.8 Turn hard left at a switchback, climbing the woods road. Soon the trail will pass a "3 Mile" marker.

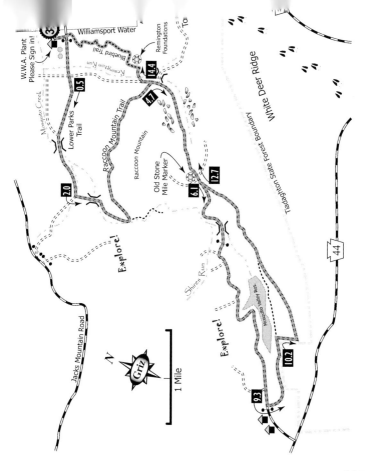

W.W.A. Plant
Please Sign in!

Williamsport Water

Remington Foundations

To

3

0.5

14.4

4.7

Bluebird Trail

Remington Run

Mosquito Creek

Lower Parks Trail

Raccoon Mountain Trail

Raccoon Mountain

Old Stone Mile Marker

2.0

Explore!

6.1

12.7

Shires Run

Mosquito Valley Run

Explore!

White Deer Ridge

Tiadaghton State Forest Boundary

44

Jacks Mountain Road

N

Griz

1 Mile

10.2

9.3

1.7 Turn right at the T intersection on to the woods road. Soon after pass a left spur trail and bridge that leads to Heller Reservoir.

6.1 Pass old stone mile marker stating "Mile 7, WILLIAMPORT" and a 4 way intersection. Continue straight as the woods road soon descends, crossing Mosquito Creek in a metal-grate bridge at mile 6.9.

7.1 Pass around a green metal gate as the trail continues to climb passing a few side roads.

9.3 Turn left just before the gated road, following the grassy road as it parallels an old stone wall.

10.2 Either way works here! For mileage purposes, turn right at the right spur woods road and climb. Soon after (mile 10.4) the trail turns 90 degrees left.

12.7 Merge right on the woods road as the trail passes the stone mile-marker again and descends.

Old stone mile-mark

14.4 After passing the Raccoon Mountain Trail on the left, turn right on to the Bluebird Trail, marked by a "Bluebird" icon and wooden sign. As the grade climbs, the trail passes the Remington Estate ruins on the right (mile 14.6). Continue to follow the "Bluebird" icons on the trees.

15.8 Cross Mosquito Valley Road to the trailhead. Don't forget to sign out at the trailhead, our access to this beautiful area depends on our compliance!

.... west along the river to Douboistown. In the heart of the very small town of Doubiostown, turn left on to Valley Road. Valley Road is easy to miss and best identified by an Exxon Mini Market gas station on one corner and on the adjacent corner, the Valley Inn restaurant. Travel 0.6 miles along Valley Road and turn left on Mosquito Valley Road, which is also marked with a steel sign stating the 'Williamsport Water Authority'. Soon after keep left at the road fork. Take this road 1.6 miles to a dead-end turn-around, and pass through the gate into the Williamsport Water Authority. Turn right and park in the gravel parking area, denoted by the wooden sign. You must sign in at the building entrance. **GPS**: N41-11.965' W77-2.590'

Distance: 6.3 mile loop

Time: 1-2 hours

Highlights: Excellent casual ride in a beautiful 'preserve', incredible wildlife viewing

Technical Difficulty: 1. The entire ride follows dirt service. The roads vary in tread from gravel to dirt to grass with little in the way of technical challenges.

Aerobic Difficulty: Easy. The midpoint of the ride is also the high-point of the ride with a gentle three-mile climb to get you there. The trail surfaces are smooth and fast, making this loop an easy cruise.

Vertical: 665 feet of climbing

Climbing Distance: 3.2 miles

Maps: USGS Williamsport

Land Status: Williamsport Water Authority

Ride Notes: The Williamsport Water Authority is a little known secret tucked away in the hills south of Williamsport proper. The

WWA is huge tract of land that was acquired to protect and preserve the water watershed that supplies water to the Williamsport area. Within this massive land track there are 2 large reservoirs, the Mosquito Valley and Heller reservoirs. These two impoundments are closed to any kind of water recreation due to the sensitive nature of the resource as drinking water. I must admit that the lakes are quite placid and peerin, due to the 100 yard posted perimeter restriction placed upon them. Plenty of deer, grouse, turkey, porcupine, and bear abound in this protected area. This haven is home to many of these and other critters, which may offer a photographic opportunity so don't forget the camera.

The ride begins at the WWA Treatment Facility building where riders need to sign-in on the clipboard at the building entrance. From here a quick spin on the pavement and around a gate will send you down the dirt 'country' road. A left turn begins the slow and gradual climb to the Raccoon Mountain Trail, along beautiful stands of mixed hardwoods. The trail turns sharply, continuing the climb on the east shoulder of Raccoon Mountain and traverses the north face. An old spring seeps from the mountain, encased in stonework from long ago. The ride reaches the apex on the mountain and begins the fun payback descent. A switchbacked trail soon crosses Mosquito Creek on a modern concrete bridge as the ride rolls down to another old stone bridge. This ancient span is accompanied by some backcountry humor, a wooden sign stating the possible presence of a toll-keeping Troll. The final stretch spins out to trailhead on well-maintained dirt roads and finishes at the WWA treatment plant. Don't forget to sign out at the trailhead, the access to this beautiful area depends on our compliance!

THE RIDE...

0.0 Head out from the parking area, sign in, and turn right at the T on Mosquito Valley Road. Pass around a gate and continue on the dirt road.

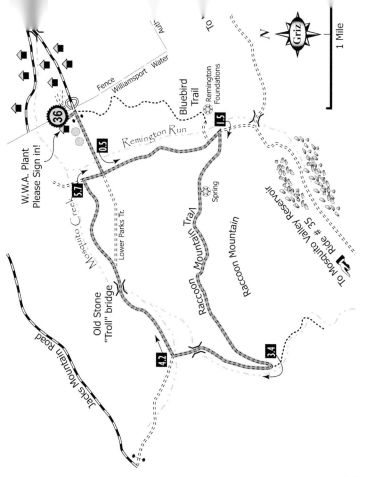

N

Griz

1 Mile

TO

Bluebird Trail

⊗ Remington Foundations

1.5

Fence Williamsport Water

Remington Run

0.5

36

W.W.A. Plant
Please Sign in!

5.7

Mosquito Creek

Lower Parks Tr.

Spring ⊗

Raccoon Mountain Trail

Raccoon Mountain

To Mosquito Valley Reservoir

To Mosquito Valley Ride # 35

Old Stone
"Troll" bridge

Jacks Mountain Road

4.2

3.4

0.5 Turn left at the 4-way intersection.

1.3 Turn hard right on the Raccoon Mountain Trail and continue to climb. Soon you will pass an old stone-encased spring on the left.

3.4 Turn hard right at the sharp switchback in the road, continuing to descend

3.9 Cross a concrete bridge over Mosquito Creek.

4.2 Turn (bear) right at a T intersection, continuing to descend

4.8 Ride over the old stone bridge with a classic "Troll" sign posted nearby.

5.0 Keep left at the fork.

5.7 Turn right at the T intersection and soon after (mile 5.8) turn left at the 4-way intersection.

6.3 Pass around the gate and turn left into the trailhead parking area. Please sign out!

Do like the sign says...for fear he might steal your ride!

State Highway 654 west along the river to Douboistown. In the heart of the very small town of Doubiostown, turn left on to Valley Road. Valley Road is easy to miss and best identified by an Exxon Mini Market gas station on one corner and on the adjacent corner, the Valley Inn restaurant. Travel 0.6 miles along Valley Road and turn left on Mosquito Valley Road, which is also marked with a steel sign stating the 'Williamsport Water Authority'. Soon after keep left at the road fork. Take this road 1.6 miles to a dead-end turn-around, and pass through the gate into the Williamsport Water Authority. Turn right and park in the gravel parking area, denoted by the wooden sign. You must sign in at the building entrance. **GPS**: N41-11.965' W77-2.590'

Distance: 13.8 mile loop with an out and back section.

Time: 2-4 hours.

Highlights: Remote riding in a 'sanctuary' setting, excellent wildlife viewing, a true 'oasis' just outside of town, mellow ride for energetic folks of all abilities.

Technical Difficulty: **1**. The route follows awesome woods roads that are relatively smooth and hardpacked. The novice rider will enjoy the smoother tread through the woods and the experienced rider will appreciate the fast surface the route provides.

Aerobic Difficulty: **Easy to Moderate**. The ride slowly climbs up through a gap and then descends down along the lake to the dam breast. The ride then retraces much of the route before looping up and around Raccoon Mountain on a mild climb and final descent to the trailhead.

Vertical: 2,402 feet of climbing

Climbing Distance: 8.2 miles

Maps: USGS Williamsport

Land Status: Williamsport Water Authority

Ride Notes: The Williamsport Water Authority tract is an oasis just outside of town and is a true haven for critters and humans alike. This spectacular refuge is open for mountain biking which allows you to explore this vast area by means of pedal power. The great mountain ride is probably the most fun and mellow true mountain ride in the area. A great introductory ride for aspiring mountain families due to the smooth trail surface, this ride really takes you 'away from it all'. Beginning at the treatment plant (after signing in!) the ride spins out on country-style dirt roads as it slowly climbs to a bridge over Remington Run. More climbing follows as the route winds its way out to the Heller Reservoir. Along the tranquil shores of the lake, it's often possible to spot many forms of wildlife from deer to waterfowl. Please observe the posted 'border' around the reservoir as the impound serves as a water source to the city. The ride cruises along the exposed rim of the earthen dam and crosses the confluence where it terminates at State Highway 554. From here the ride retraces its way back to Remington Run and begins a loop on Raccoon Mountain. A fun climb starts out a bit steep but soon mellows out as the ride then descends the mountain and rambles back to the trailhead.

THE RIDE...

0.0 Head out from the parking area, sign in, and turn right at the T on Mosquito Valley Road. Pass around a gate and continue on the dirt road.

0.5 Turn left at the 4-way intersection.

1.5 Pass Raccoon Mountain Trail on the right. Soon after (mile 1.7) turn left on to a gated dirt road, which crosses Remington Run on a green steel bridge.

3.3 Keep left at the fork, the right fork is off-limits to all.

194

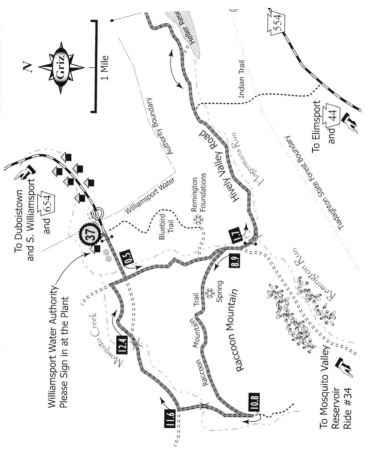

N Griz

1 Mile

Heller Res

554

Indian Trail

To Elimsport and 44

Tiadaghton State Forest Boundary

Williamsport Water Authority Boundary

To Duboistown and S. Williamsport and 654

Williamsport Water Authority Please Sign in at the Plant

37

Remington Foundations

Bluebird Trail

Hilvey Valley Road

Flagstonais Run

0.5

8.9

1.1

12.4

Mosquito Creek

Raccoon Mountain Trail

Spring

Raccoon Mountain

Remington Run

11.6

10.8

To Mosquito Valley Reservoir Ride #34

195

4.6 Pass under the power line. Soon after turn right at a right spur, crossing the dam breast.

4.8 Cross the spillway by either means, following the gravel road around left.

5.2 Arrive at the gate on State Highway 554. Turn around and retrace your route back across the girder steel bridge (mile 8.7) and the Raccoon Mountain Trail

8.9 Turn left on to Raccoon Mountain Trail and climb the woods road.

9.4 Pass a small rock structure built around a spring, on the left.

10.8 Turn hard right at a switchback.

11.3 Cross over Mosquito Creek on a concrete decked bridge.

11.6 Turn right at the T intersection.

12.4 Pass over the old stone bridge with the wooden 'Troll' sign that offers a little backwoods humor! Soon after keep left at the fork.

13.1 Turn right at the T and soon after (mile 13.3) turn left at the 4-way intersection. Follow this back to the trailhead.

13.8 The final stretch spins out to trailhead on dirt roads to finish at the WWA treatment plant. Don't forget to sign out at the trailhead, our access to this beautiful area depends on our compliance!

Left & Top: Heller Reservoir   **Bottom:** Wild Turkey chick hiding out

CAMPING OUT

Many State Parks with overnight and day use facilities are found through the region. The State Forest allows primitive camping in designated areas. All State Park facilities have restrooms and some have water, which may be seasonal. State Forest campsites do not have water or restroom facilities and you must practice 'pack-in, pack-out'. The following are a list of places for those willing to 'rough-it' in the true beauty of Penns Woods. The contact phone number for all Pennsylvania State Parks is 1-800-PAPARKS.

NORTHERN BALD EAGLE REGION

Bald Eagle State Forest- The Bald Eagle has designated over 40 specific camping site throughout the entire forest. Each roadside campsite is equipped with a large steel fire ring with cooking grate. No water or restroom facilities are provided. Camping is free but a permit is required before camping at any of these locations. Contact the Bald Eagle State Forest office headquarters in Laurelton Center at 570-922-3344 for camp location maps, forestry camping rules, fire-ban and permit information.

R.B. Winter State Park- R.B. Winter has over 60 campsites, some of which are equiped with electric hook-up. There are a few cabins for rent and the park has also added an awesome shower house facility which is included in the campsite fee. The chilly, spring-fed 7-acre lake offers fishing and swimming.

McCall Dam State Park- McCall Dam area is actuall a trailhead location for a few rides in the guide and offers organized group camping at this primitive site. The location also offers great trout fishing along the White Deer Creek, which runs through the park.

Bald Eagle State Forest- The Bald Eagle has designated over 40 specific camping site throughout the entire forest. Each roadside campsite is equipped with a large steel fire ring with cooking grate. No water or restroom facilities are provided. Camping is free but a permit is required before camping at any of these locations. Contact the Bald Eagle State Forest office headquarters in Laurelton Center at 570-922-3344 for camp location maps, forestry camping rules, fire-ban and permit information.

Poe Valley State Park- Poe Valley offers 76 campsites. The 35-acre lake offers fishing, boating boat rentals and swimming.

Poe Paddy State Park- Poe Paddy has over 40 campsites and a few 3-sided shelters. Penns Creek, the world renowned limestone trout stream, runs through this location offering swimming and fishing.

Reeds Gap State Park- Reeds Gap offers 14 tent campsites. A swimming pool and nearby fishing stream are some park highlights.

Penn Roosevelt State Park- A few primitive self-pay campsites are available at this location, which is located in the Rothrock State Forest. A small pond provides some fishing. Contact Greenwood Furnace State Park at 814-667-1800 for more information.

DED AND BREAKFAST

For those looking for a bit more comfort (hot showers and warm meals), the area B&B's are an intimate alternative to the camping scene. Beautiful homes on estates with manicured properties set in incredibly locations make your mountain bike outing that much more enjoyable. These establishments come highly recommended and truly cater to the outdoors and cycling enthusiasts. This place is not only their business location but their backyard as well. Nobody knows the local attractions better than the locals themselves. The hospitality of these folks is second to none and in the morning they're sure to send you out into the woods with a good nites rest and a hearty stokin' breakfast!

Centre Mills

Bed & Breakfast on Elk Creek in Centre County, PA

Step back in time and discover the pleasures of a wonderful 26-acre estate located on the western edge of Bald Eagle State Forest. Centre Mills offers many amenities for the visiting mountain cyclist ...

-A Spacious barn for bike storage and large decks for relaxing
-A hearty homemade country breakfast with fresh baked goods
-Excellent fly-fishing on Elk Creek on the estate premises
-Conveniently located to many of the Griz Guide rides

814-349-8000   www.centremills.com

Maria Davison - Proprietor

Bicycle Tour

The hills aren't the only things rolling in central Pennsylvania! With its gently sloping terrain and tranquil rural vistas, the Buffalo Valley has become a haven for bicyclists seeking Serendipity in the land of antiques, Amish quilts, and homemade whoopie pies. Come and explore country roads less traveled, at a leisurely pace. Revel in a three-day inn-to-inn cycling tour with stopovers at **Anni's Inn & Outings, The Inn at New Berlin, and Maison Boisée.**

Package pricing from $398.00 plus tax
(per person, double occupancy)

For more information:
www.innatnewberlin.com/biketour.htm
1-800-797-2350

www.anni-bnb.com (570-523-7163)
www.maisonboisee.com (570-922-4164)
www.visitcentralpa.org (800-525-7320)

PENNSYLVANIA | *memories last a lifetime*

OUTSIDE ADVENTURES

There is so much to do in and around the Bald Eagle State Forest. Many miles of designated hiking trail lead to unique natural areas and geologic features. Numerous limestone creeks and wide rivers are great for fishing, canoeing, kayaking and plain cooling-off. Local limestone caves explore the subterranean world below as rocky escarpments allow you the opportunity to experience the vertical world above. In winter, things freeze up for activities like ice fishing ice-skating, ice climbing and cross country skiing.

CONTACT INFORMATION

State Parks ....1-800-PAPARKS......www.dcnr.state.pa.us

Public parks ....www.dcnr.state.pa.us

Bald Eagle State Forest... 570-922-3344

Tiadaghton State Forest..................... 570-327-3450

Rothrock State Forest 814-643-2340

Pennsylvania Game Commission ....www.pgc.state.pa.us

KMBA (Keystone IMBA)..................................www.patrails

Central PA mountain bike orginizations...............www.patrails.com

FREE UPDATES and downloads...................www.grizguides.com

Choclate  **Helmet**

Mountain biking in Pennsylvania is a year-round activity. Summers are sometimes hot and humid. Finding a ride near a lake or stream is your best bet on a hot day. The mountains are typically cooler but at times the humidity prevails. Fall is ideal riding weather with cool nights and warm days and dry trail. Riding in the woods during the fall foliage spectacle is beyond description. The leaves typically reach the height of brilliance during the 2nd and 3rd week in October. Winter brings yet another change as the mountains funnel weather along their flanks. Winter weather is sometimes dry yet it is not uncommon to get altitude-affected snows. Heavy snows last a while in these mountains and north and east facing slopes keep the snow cover longer. Spring is usually wet, making riding on certain trails an issue of concern. Please stay off of wet trails for erosion purposes, as the soils are very sensitive. Spring is also the height of the fire season due to the high winds and the heavy amount of dead leaves so be real careful with campfires. Call the State Forest before heading out, to check on fire-bans in effect during any season.

great
outdoors

Create your own adventure on the
more than 2.4 million acres of state
forest and park lands. Free access.
Year round. Pure fun. Explore.

www.dcnr.state.pa.us

DCNR

The Pennsylvania Department of
Conservation and Natural Resources

Appendix

SHORT LIST O' RIDES

Lazy Riders
2. Pine Swamp
5. Penns Valley Rail Trail West
6. Penns Valley Rail Trail East
14. Round Top Mountain Lookout
16. Bear Mountain
17. Hall Mountain Trail
18. Rapid Run Ramble
36. Raccoon Mountain
37. Heller Reservior.

Mild n' Mellow:
3. Big Poe Mountain
8. Bull Hollow
10. Middle Ridge to Henstep Valley
19. Hough Mountain Trail
23. Boiling Springs
29. Heintz Trail to Swenks Gap

Mettleing Moderates:
1. Wildcat Gap to Faust Valley
13. Shade Mountain
15. Big Mountain
22. Fallen Timber Trail
25. Old Tram Trail
31. Dynamite Shack
34. Mountain Gap Trail
35. Mosquito Valley

Shout o' Stout:
11. Penns Creek Mountain
12. Boonoy Mountain
21. Douty Mill trail
28. Mags Path
33. Sand Spring Flat

Epics:
4. Seven Mountains Enduro Epic
7. Tunnel Mountain Trail
9. Strong Mountain
20. Sharpback to Rocky Corner
24. Cowbell Hollow
26. Buffalo Mountain
30. Spike Buck to Top Mountain
32. Southern Tiadaghton Tour

Gravity!

HANDBUILT IN THE ROCKIES IS ONLY THE HALF OF IT

Achieving Moots craftsmanship and art will always come down to the details of the process. What good is the agony of precise miters, machined fittings and parts, and our har selected titanium tubing, if we don't understand its val and feel on the trail. This process drives outcome. Torch. Test. Repeat. Moots...

Moots. Custom built titanium in Steamboat Springs, Colorado.
www.moots.com

MOOT

ABOUT THE AUTHOR

From backcountry alpine climbs in places like the Wind River Range WY. to solitary singletrack stretches in Steamboat, CO, I've always been drawn back 'home'... to Pennsylvania. With friends that have wandered West, I often wonder whether they ever really got to experience the essence of Penn's Woods. I must admit that the East coast pace is enough to drive any sane person West. Pennsylvania holds a special place in my soul, an intimacy that is unmatched. With a passion for just plain being outside, I enjoy sharing my experiences and the incredible places I've been to, which is why I write. My guidebooks are a part of my soul and within them, embodies my spirit. I believe that the mountains yield a special energy from which I willingly harvest... ride hard, wander free, live long!

"Look to the mountains, it's there you'll find it"

GUY'S BICYCLES.COM

Bicycles -We stock a diverse array of mountain, road, hybrid and BMX bikes, including a special 'pro-shop' with high-end bikes. **FREE** assembly of all bikes and **FREE** brake and gear adjustments for an entire year after your purchase!

Parts and Accessories -The "If we don't have it, we'll get it" attitude at Guy's has earned us a reputation for outstanding service...though we can usually answer even the rarest of parts and accessory requests with existing inventory.

Specialty Service -We take great pride in the specialized services we offer and use our experience to fill your needs accurately and efficiently...from simple repairs to custom bicycle fittings.

Community Support -For more than 25 years Guy's Bicycles has supported the local cycling community. We've had the opportunity to promote the area's finest BMX, Road, MTB, and Triathlete Teams.

Stop by our shop...

or visit us online at:
guysbicycles.com

326 East Street Road
Feasterville, PA 19053
215.355.1166

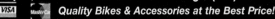

N.M.B.A

Nittany Mountain Biking Association

"To preserve, protect, and improve
the trails we love."

www.NittanyMBA.net

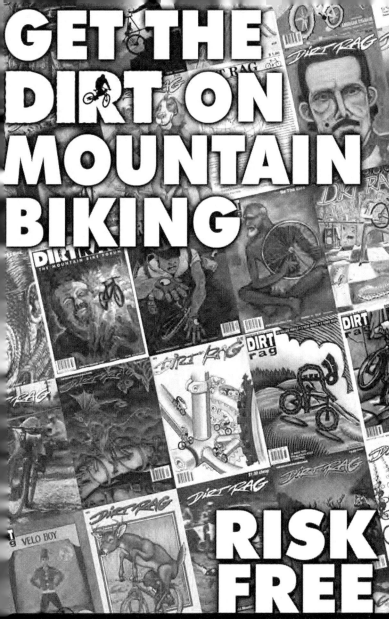

GET THE DIRT ON MOUNTAIN BIKING

RISK FREE

DIRTRAG is the mountain bike forum, an independent magazine written by and for real mountain bikers...

Just like YOU!

Dirt Rag brings you down-to-earth, honest and insightful coverage of the sport you love...

- Honest product reviews.
- Practical tips for maintenance and repairs.
- Skill and riding techniques.
- Cool places to ride.
- Nationwide event calendar.
- Free product raffle in every issue.
- Expert advice.

Find out why our readers call us *the heart and soul of mountain biking!*

Send for your FREE ISSUE today!

☑ **Yes!** Please rush my **FREE ISSUE** of *Dirt Rag* magazine and enter a trial subscription in my name. If I like *Dirt Rag*, I can get a full year (seven more issues for a total of eight) for only $16.95—a savings of 39% off the newsstand price. If I'm not completely satisfied, I'll write cancel on the bill and owe nothing. The **FREE ISSUE** is mine to keep.

Print your name and address below.

SEND NO MONEY
Limited Time Offer
Offer valid in North America only.

NAME:

ADDRESS:

CITY: STATE: ZIP:

Detach and return this order form today to:
Dirt Rag Free Offer, 3483 Saxonburg Blvd., Pittsburgh, PA 15238   Code: Griz002